MY LIFE AND WORK

By
ALEXANDER WALTERS

First Fruits Press
Wilmore, Kentucky
c2016

My life and work.
By Alexander Walters.

First Fruits Press, ©2016
Previously published by Felming H. Revell Company, ©1917.

ISBN: 9781621715535 (print) 9781621715542 (digital) 9781621715559 (kindle)

Digital version at http://place.asburyseminary.edu/firstfruitsheritagematerial/133/

First Fruits Press is a digital imprint of the Asbury Theological Seminary, B.L. Fisher Library. Asbury Theological Seminary is the legal owner of the material previously published by the Pentecostal Publishing Co. and reserves the right to release new editions of this material as well as new material produced by Asbury Theological Seminary. Its publications are available for noncommercial and educational uses, such as research, teaching and private study. First Fruits Press has licensed the digital version of this work under the Creative Commons Attribution Noncommercial 3.0 United States License. To view a copy of this license, visit http://creativecommons.org/licenses/by-nc/3.0/us/.

For all other uses, contact:

First Fruits Press
B.L. Fisher Library
Asbury Theological Seminary
204 N. Lexington Ave.
Wilmore, KY 40390
http://place.asburyseminary.edu/firstfruits

Walters, Alexander, 1858-1917

My life and work / by Alexander Walters.
Wilmore, Kentucky : First Fruits Press, ©2016.
272 pages : illustrations, portraits ; 21 cm.

Reprint. Previously published: New York ; Toronto : Fleming H. Revell Company, ©1917.
ISBN - 13: 9781621715535 (pbk.)

1. Walters, Alexander, 1858- 2. African Methodist Episcopal Zion Church--Bishops--Biography. 3. African American clergy—Biography. 4. Slaves--Kentucky--Biography I. Title.

BX8473.W3 A3 2016

Cover design by Jonathan Ramsay

asburyseminary.edu
800.2ASBURY
204 North Lexington Avenue
Wilmore, Kentucky 40390

First Fruits Press
The Academic Open Press of Asbury Theological Seminary
204 N. Lexington Ave., Wilmore, KY 40390
859-858-2236
first.fruits@asburyseminary.edu
asbury.to/firstfruits

MY LIFE AND WORK

MY LIFE AND WORK

BY

ALEXANDER WALTERS, A.M., D.D.

Bishop of the African Methodist Episcopal Zion Church

ILLUSTRATED

NEW YORK   CHICAGO   TORONTO

Fleming H. Revell Company

LONDON   AND   EDINBURGH

Copyright, 1917, by
FLEMING H. REVELL COMPANY

New York : 158 Fifth Avenue
Chicago : 17 North Wabash Ave.
Toronto : 25 Richmond Street, W.
London : 21 Paternoster Square
Edinburgh: 100 Princes Street

DEDICATION

TO THE

MINISTERS AND LAYMEN OF THE A. M. E. ZION CHURCH,
WHO HAVE BEEN SO VERY KIND TO ME
DURING MY MINISTERIAL CAREER,
I AFFECTIONATELY DEDICATE THIS VOLUME,
HOPING IT MAY BE OF BENEFIT TO
THE RISING GENERATION.

INTRODUCTION

KING ALFONSO was wont to say, dead counsellors (meaning his books) were to him far better than living; for they without flattery or fear presented to him truth.

There is no end of books; many libraries are purchased for sight and ostentation rather than use. Some one has cruelly observed that a good many people, including some of the newly rich, buy their books by the yard, and to match the furniture. A few books well chosen and well made use of will be more profitable than a great confused Alexandrian Library.

Bishops as a rule have little time to write books, for their work is often of such character that they either cannot spare the time, or they have not the inclination to think or write upon subjects outside of their special work, and particularly is this true of some of our Negro Bishops. There are a few notable exceptions, such as Bishops Daniel A. Payne, Jas. W. Hood, Benjamin T. Tanner and Henry McNeal Turner. All of these are men of exceptional literary ability, men of strong characters, men with a message. They write well and learnedly on church polity and discipline and on related subjects. Payne, Hood, Tanner and Turner have done much to give character, prominence and tone to Negro Methodism in America.

Their books on Church History, Church Discipline, and Church Ethics have been and still are widely read. Tanner's apology for "African Methodism" cuts like a two-edged sword, for it is more than an apology—it is an indictment with all the evidence, against the caste and color prejudices of the white Methodist brethren—their refusal to acknowledge the Fatherhood of God, and the brotherhood of man. It detracts nothing from Negro Methodism, but it is a terrible reflection upon the genuineness of the religion of white men in that church. It is a protest against hyprocrisy phrased in dignified terms, an "apology" with a punch and a jolt to it which those to whom it is specially addressed will not fail to understand. Payne and Hood and Turner also wrote in serious vein. Payne was velvet; Hood was a pacificator; Turner a whirlwind and Niagara combined. This quartette is still the principal authority in America on Negro Methodism, what constitutes it, and what ought to govern and control in this great Negro Methodist family. They are the pioneers in our later civilization of African Methodism and have written their names on the hearts and in the memories of thousands of Negro Methodists throughout the world as defenders and exponents of the faith once delivered unto the Saints.

And now the Rt. Rev. Alexander Walters, the youngest Bishop in either branch of the great African Methodist Church, a man widely and favorably known in his own country, in Europe

INTRODUCTION 11

and in Africa,—a man of recognized ability as an orator and pulpiteer of liberal ideas and generous impulses,—has written "The Autobiography of Alexander Walters," covering a period of forty years of activity in the church as layman, local preacher, minister and Bishop—the highest office in the gift of his Church. Forty years of active, useful, honorable service to his Creator, and to his race, and his country; forty years filled with thrilling and pleasant experiences—of lights and shadows—of ups and downs,—the lot of the average clergyman of every denomination. What a glory is this to have lived and worked in the cause of humanity, oppressed for forty years! To have known and fellowshipped with great and good and useful men of four continents, to have mingled in splendid alliance with the old veterans of the Grand Army of the living God and joined with them in making their ascriptions to the Giver of all good, both in the land of his birth, and that of his forefathers in the "Dark Continent," from whence the light proceedeth which will ultimately fill all the world with the vitalizing, purifying power of the Holy Spirit, which is to revolutionize Christian thought and teach men what true and undefiled religion is and means. For the African being the most spiritual race has a mission and it is to carry the gospel in all its purity and completeness and power to those who know not God.

The "Autobiography of Alexander Walters" is a departure and innovation in Negro literature in that it is *different* from the usual run of autobiographies. It is a combination of church history, race history, a delicate kind of humor, tragedy and pathos. We are told that the Bishop was born in slavery, Aug. 1, 1858, in Nelson County, Kentucky, a picturesque section of the "Blue Grass" region; that his mother, Harriet Mathers Walters, was a woman of prodigious size, well built and weighing 250 lbs. She was strong, active, courageous; a terror to her master and others, who dreaded her because of her physical prowess. A story is told of her which illustrates the point: One day her master and his son got into an altercation about some trivial matter and almost came to blows. Happening along when the wordy battle was raging at its hottest, and sensing the situation quickly, she seized her young master by the nape of his neck and the broadest part of his trousers, lifted him off his feet and shaking him as a cat shakes a mouse, tossed him over into the grape arbor. Shamed by this humiliating ending of the controversy with his father, he gathered himself up and meekly left the scene.

Her mistress, Mrs. Donohue, was very fond of her and a warm attachment existed between them. Harriet was obstreperous and unmanageable, and because she was different in these respects from other slaves, she was regarded as dangerous. Her influence over her fellow slaves was not conducive to that sweet contentment born of the cat o' nine tails, the gibbet and other cruel methods employed

INTRODUCTION 13

by "good masters" to produce this desideratum in the home, so it was decided to sell Harriet and, without consulting his wife, Donohue sold her to a trader for $1200. When Mrs. Donohue learned of the sale, she approached the Negro trader and shaking her finger in his face, and stamping her foot with emphasis, said: "Harriet shall never leave this place." And she didn't, for the sale was declared off and Harriet resumed her household duties as usual. Alexander Walters owes much to his slave mother—his splendid physique, his personal courage, his independence of spirit, his deep religious fervor and his ambition to excel in whatever he undertook. His good mother knew no fear, for she was more than a match for any three men in physical strength on the place, and whenever they roused her she put the fear of God in their hearts.

The Bishop's narrative is told in modest phrase and in simple language and covers twenty-one chapters which are bound to hold the readers' attention because of the manner in which the various topics treated are discussed. In chapter I, we get a glimpse of Bardstown, its people and incidents which recall to memory the happy days of yore. Bardstown is dear to the Bishop's heart—here are memories and associations which cannot be effaced and to these he pays the tribute of love and veneration, for it is his "Old Kentucky Home," and the fragrant odor of the magnolia and the wild rose lingers in memory's casket.

There is not a dull page in the book, as any one acquainted with the Bishop might know on seeing his name as its author, for he is not a dull nor uninteresting man to talk with, or to read after. He has the happy faculty of holding one's attention whether in private conversation or preaching a sermon, or communicating his views through the press. I have examined very carefully the MSS. of the book and I am able to commend it to the reader as a book as worthy of perusal as it is of the big-hearted, whole-souled, generous man, who has taken the public into his confidence and told it his life story in charming, but simple phrase. He has wrought exceedingly well.

John Edward Bruce.

CONTENTS

		PAGE
I.	ANCESTRY AND BIRTH	19
II.	YOUTHFUL DAYS	28
III.	EARLY RELIGIOUS IMPRESSIONS, CONVERSION, ETC.	34
IV.	EXPERIENCES IN LOUISVILLE	38
V.	AT THE GOLDEN GATE	44
VI.	CHATTANOOGA AND KNOXVILLE	50
VII.	THE GREAT METROPOLIS	53
VIII.	EUROPE	57
IX.	EGYPT AND THE HOLY LAND	70
X.	HOME AGAIN	83
XI.	THE CENTENNIAL JUBILEE	89
XII.	THE AFRO-AMERICAN COUNCIL	95
XIII.	GENERAL CONFERENCES	141
XIV.	MY TRIP TO WEST COAST OF AFRICA	149
XV.	INDEPENDENCE IN POLITICS	177
XVI.	WORK IN THE UNITED SOCIETY OF CHRISTIAN ENDEAVOR	199
XVII.	ADDRESS AT ALEXANDRA PALACE, LONDON	219
XVIII.	THE CHICAGO CHRISTIAN ENDEAVOR CONVENTION, 1915	233
XIX.	ECUMENICAL CONFERENCES	247
XX.	THE PAN-AFRICAN CONFERENCE	253
XXI.	METHODIST UNITY	265

ILLUSTRATIONS

	OPPOSITE PAGE
ALEXANDER WALTERS................*Frontispiece*	
DONAHOE HOTEL, NOW THE NEWMAN HOUSE. In the kitchen of this house Bishop Walters was born	20
FIRST SCHOOLHOUSE AND CHURCH ATTENDED BY BISHOP WALTERS...................	38
THE HOUSE IN WHICH MRS. LELIA WALTERS WAS BORN............................	54
MRS. LELIA WALTERS......................	72
NEW CHURCH TO WHICH BISHOP WALTERS CONTRIBUTED THE FIRST $25..........	178
THE OLD MILL AT BARDSTOWN.............	254

I

ANCESTRY AND BIRTH

"My bark is wafted to the strand
  By breath divine;
And on the helm there rests a hand
  Other than mine."
—DEAN OF CANTERBURY.

THE patriotic Italian delights to speak of his far-famed country, with its soft blue skies, famous churches, and renowned cities, one of which is so beautiful that it is said of it, "See Naples and die." The Frenchman never tires of boasting of Versailles and its wonderful palace, built by Louis XIV, which cost such an enormous sum of money that the king was afraid to show the receipts to his Cabinet. The Englishman points with pride to Stratford-on-Avon, the home of Shakespeare, the world's greatest poet. The American is equally proud of Mt. Vernon, the home of Washington, "Father of his country"; and we Kentuckians believe our State to be the garden spot of the world. It was one of our famous authors who said, "When God Almighty created the heavens and the earth, He made the little birds to sing, the flowers to bloom, the sun to shine and nature all grand and beautiful. He made Kentucky the garden spot of the universe and Nelson County the heart thereof."

Nelson County is delightfully situated in the North-central part of Kentucky; its towering and majestic hills stand out like grim sentinels in the southern and western part of the county,—the county where all is peace, challenging the whole world to compete with it in grandeur and scenic beauty."

"Where the sky is pure as azure
And the forest nature's green;
Where the valleys meet the hilltops
And the earth is clothed in sheen.

Where fruits and grains are plenteous
And the crystal waters prime.
This is Nelson County's picture
As it looks in simple rhyme."

It was at Federal Hill, near Bardstown, in old Nelson County, that Stephen Collins Foster wrote "My Old Kentucky Home"—words and melody that will live as long as the English language is spoken; sentiments that will ever cheer and inspire Kentuckians in any part of the world.

Bardstown, the county seat of old Nelson, is the third oldest city in Kentucky, having been founded in 1774. Situated on a prominent knoll overlooking the Bardstown creek, in the centre of the most fertile agricultural district, an enchanting location, lies this historic old town. In this city stands

DONAHOE HOTEL, NOW THE NEWMAN HOUSE
In the kitchen of this house Bishop Walters was born

ANCESTRY AND BIRTH 21

the famous St. Joseph's College of the Roman Catholic Church, from whose classic walls have gone forth some of the most distinguished men of that faith. In addition to these, many famous men are proud to call Bardstown their birthplace.

Among such may be mentioned Ben Hardin, the great lawyer; Judge John Rowan, Charles Anderson Wickliffe, Hon. Felix Grundy, noted jurists; John Fitch, the inventor of the steamboat; Governor William Johnson, Charles Davis Pennybaker, great orators; Col. W. M. Beckham; his son, Hon. J. C. W. Beckham, the present governor; the gifted Judge Grisby, and others.

Louis Philippe, the exile king of France, resided here for about a year, and afterwards made several valuable presents to St. Joseph's Church, which, by the way, is the most historical, as well as one of the most beautiful, Catholic churches in the State. Among the most interesting buildings in the city of Bardstown is the old tavern in which I was born; the old Court House opposite the tavern, the old brown water-mill below the city, the little old church in which I went to school; and the new Zion Church to build which I contributed the first twenty-five dollars. The colored Baptist church is the oldest church building in the city occupied by Negroes, and for a long while the Baptists and the Methodists used this church as a Union Meeting House. Later the Methodists withdrew and worshipped in the little frame school house.

In this old historic Kentucky town, one Sunday

morning, the first of August, 1858, in a room in the rear of the kitchen of the Donohue Hotel, now the Newman House, I first beheld the light of day. My father, Henry Walters, was born in Larue County, of sturdy old Kentucky stock, the son of his master, in whose veins flowed the bluest blood of the State. I am told on good authority that my father was a distant relative of Abraham Lincoln. My father lived to the ripe age of eighty-five years, after a life characterized by a serene and hopeful spirit, leaving a memory fragrant with the Christian graces.

My mother was Harriet Mathers, a native of Virginia, and from the best information I could secure from my father, I learned that she belonged to John Dixon of Missouri, who is thought to have married into the family of her first owners. Mr. Dixon moved from Missouri to Larue County, Kentucky, and she passed out of his hands into those of a family named Mathers, living in the same county. Later she became the property of Michael Donohue, of Bardstown, Kentucky. My mother was tall and commanding in figure, of a light brown complexion and the embodiment of energy. She weighed over two hundred pounds and possessed unusual strength for a woman.

On one occasion, when her master and his son were in a fight, the son seemed to have the advantage and was about to stab his father with a butcher knife. Mother heard the struggle and rushed in to see what was the matter. On beholding the situation, she seized her young master,

ANCESTRY AND BIRTH

weighing one hundred and fifty pounds, by the seat of his trousers and the nape of his neck, carried him to the kitchen door and threw him into the grape arbor, about six feet away. Though he suffered no bodily injury, you can imagine he suffered much humiliation and chagrin.

My mother was as brave as a lion: she would not brook even an unjust reprimand from her master. On one occasion when the breakfast was late, her master took her severely to task. She, knowing the abuse was unmerited, resented his harshness and threw the rolling-pin at him. For this grave offense she was condemned to be sold.

The day of the sale arrived, and the negro-traders were on hand. Among the buyers was a vicious-looking fellow by the name of Mac-Donald. When mother was put up for sale, the bidding started off at five hundred dollars, and after a spirited contest, she was knocked down to MacDonald for one thousand dollars. At this juncture, the mistress of the home, who had been a silent observer of the sale, stepped forward and said to the master: "Mike, Harriet can't leave this home; she belongs to me. Mother gave her to me when we were both children; we have grown up together, and, notwithstanding she has a bad temper, she is honest and industrious, and I am not going to let her go." "But," said the master, "she has been sold, hence we must let her go."

Her mistress, who weighed only about one hundred and twenty pounds, drew herself to her full height and said, "I don't care anything about that; she'll never leave this home.'' The kindness and firmness of this little woman enabled our mother to remain with her children until we were emancipated.

Mother was an enthusiastic Methodist. Many a morning at five o'clock we children were awakened by the earnest prayers and loud exclamations of praise on the part of our mother. One of my earliest church recollections was a visit to that old brick meeting house. The meeting got warm, and, as she used to say, she got warm with the meeting and began to cry and shout. I thought some one had done something to her, and I began to cry also and to hang on to her skirts, but she soon shook me loose and had her own good time. She died in 1870 in the full triumph of faith.

Our family consisted of eight children and the father and mother. Henry, the eldest son, was born in 1850; Joseph and Charles, twins, were born in 1852; John, in 1854; Isaac Burkes, in 1855; Alexander, in 1858; George Anna, in 1866; Caroline, in 1869; of these children, Joseph, Charles, John and Caroline died in infancy.

In giving these particulars concerning my family, it is with the hope that should the book fall into the hands of any one acquainted with any of my mother's relatives, they may communicate with me and through them I might be able to locate some of my long-lost relatives on my mother's side.

Next to my parents were Uncle Billy Hardin and Aunt Mahala, his wife. He was owned by the

ANCESTRY AND BIRTH

renowned Ben Hardin, the famous jurist, and was either his son or his nephew. He was the most intelligent man of color in our community. Aunt Mahala was owned by Mike Donohue, and was one of the loveliest and best women I ever knew. She was a grandmother to us children; in fact, she partly reared us. To her we would go with our sorrows, especially if mother had whipped us; we would be sure to receive comfort and consolation. She was the embodiment of kindness, one of those rare creatures who know how to soothe and make you forget your troubles. She had no children of her own, but was ever and anon adopting the children of other folks, spending considerable time and money on them, often only to have them taken from her.

My present wife, Lelia Coleman Walters, is also a native of Bardstown, and if it were left for me to state who I believe to be Nelson County's best production, I would say without hesitation, Lelia Walters. She was partly educated in a Roman Catholic Convent, completing the course of the Louisville High School, taking the highest honor in a class of thirty students. Among a number of others she was also successful in passing the examination for teachers, and was again fortunate in making the highest average, receiving an appointment to teach in the Public School of Louisville, where she served nine consecutive years as principal of the Shelby Street Schools. Upon her severance with the Public Schools of Louisville to become my wife she was the first colored teacher to receive public commendation from the School Board for long, efficient and meritorious service.

Mr. G. H. Cocran, the ex-president of the Board and a member of twenty-five years consecutive standing, on making the motion to accept the resignation, said that "the retirement of this good woman from the public school service is not only a loss to the colored schools but a distinct loss to the City of Louisville." He further stated that he had watched her career since her entrance into the service and considered her one of the most efficient teachers in the service and, in every way, worthy of the great trust committed to her care. In 1895 Mrs. Walters had the good fortune to complete a business course at Coon's Commercial High School, Kansas City, Mo.; upon the reception of her diploma, the papers of that city published the fact that she was the only colored woman in the State of Missouri holding a diploma from a school for whites only.

Mrs. Walters was an extremely popular teacher, especially beloved by the patrons of her school, and considered a well-informed woman, extensively read along all lines.

On Aug. 21, 1916, Mrs. Walters received from President Wilson, by executive order, through the influence of Judge Robert Hudspeth, an appointment to a clerkship at Ellis Island, which position she has creditably filled, being commended by Commissioner Uhl for efficiency and the high order of her intelligence. For twelve years she has been President of the African Redemption Society, and during our married life has been my constant friend and faithful assistant in all my undertakings and ever a wise and safe counsellor.

II

YOUTHFUL DAYS

> "How beautiful is youth! how bright it gleams
> With its illusions, aspirations, dreams!
> Book of Beginnings, Story without End,—
> All possibilities are in its hands,
> No danger daunts it and no foe withstands."
> —LONGFELLOW.

AT an early age my brother Isaac and I were sent to a private school which was taught by Mrs. Amanda Hines, one of the most intelligent colored women of our town; she was possessed of a pleasing disposition and winning personality which endeared her to all her pupils. We remained at this school for two terms, learning our alphabet and the Three R's, along with many other useful things not included in the curriculum. In 1868 Mr. William Lawrence of Louisville took charge of the school taught in the little frame church. My father thinking him a more efficient teacher than Mrs. Hines, we were taken from the private school and sent to him. He was of distinguished appearance and a first-rate disciplinarian. After two years he was succeeded by Miss Addie Miller, who taught for the same length of time. Miss Miller was a tiny woman, of engaging manners, but unable to cope with the big boys and girls of the school.

Following Miss Miller came the teacher who made the greatest impression on my youthful mind and who did much toward directing my thoughts to the ministry as a career. This was Mr. Rowan Wickliffe of Lexington, Kentucky, a distinguished educator and race leader. Soon after his arrival he made a proposition to the two colored churches of the town to instruct without charge a boy from each church whom they might select to be educated for the ministry. This proposal was accepted and I was chosen by the A. M. E. Zion Church and Levi Evans was chosen by the Baptist Church. Mr. Wickliffe was a fine teacher, enthusiastic, magnetic, a good disciplinarian and deeply interested in the young people under his care. I could not help but be greatly benefited by him. He was a constant source of inspiration to me and did more to shape my destiny than any one with whom I had come in contact up to that time. I remained in his school four years, this being the last school I attended.

It was while attending this school that my father moved out of Bardstown into the country, which necessitated my walking five miles daily to school. I was accustomed to rise before five in the morning, do my chores and help my grandmother get breakfast, my mother having died about the time I began studying under Mr. Wickliffe. At school I was considered an apt pupil, generally standing at the head of my class, carrying off the honors. I was very studious, caring little for sports and the usual boys' pursuits. I was very serious minded, ever looking forward to the vocation which I believed was predestined for me. At the graduating exercises of my class I had the honor to be the valedictorian, an honor all the more prized since the class numbered among its members some very bright pupils. Among these were Anna Hamilton, one of the brightest scholars of our town, a born gentlewoman, who has ever exerted a wonderful influence for good; Daniel Peppers, who is a teacher at present in Nelson County. Melissa Anderson, Josie Weathers, Eliza and Amanda Tutt, Mary E. Medcalfe, Billy, Cassie and Susie Dooms, Sallie Hamilton, Clarissa Slaughter and others I remember as among my class-mates who made especially good records in school and have since given a good account of themselves in the world.

About 1875, my father moved to a farm near Hodgensville, Larue County, Kentucky, owned by Dunlap Miller, where I labored for some time, spending the winters in Louisville, working in hotels and the like. I had already, during the summer of 1871, lived awhile in Louisville and worked at the Old St. Cloud Hotel and also at the Willard Hotel.

During one of my vacations—I think it was in 1872—I went as cabin boy on the steamer *McCrady* to Brazier City, now Morgan City, La. The steamer made trips between Morgan City and New Iberia. One night, having been found

YOUTHFUL DAYS

asleep while on duty, I was summarily discharged by the captain at New Iberia without enough money to pay my way back to Morgan City; but the boys made up my fare with fifteen cents over, which enabled me to emulate the good Ben Franklin on his arrival in Philadelphia, except that I regaled myself on ginger cake and water instead of buns and water during the three days I remained in Morgan City seeking work.

I finally got work on the dock unloading ships, but owing to my physical condition and youth, I was unable to do the work. Again my steamer friends came to my aid and contributed sufficient money to pay my passage to New Orleans, where I got work on a steamer plying between New Orleans and Donaldsonville. After six or seven months of hardship, I secured employment on the steamer *Louisville,* a stern wheeler which ran between New Orleans and Cincinnati. While in New Orleans I was much affected by hearing a lady passenger sing "My Old Kentucky Home." She came out on deck where I happened to be at work, and judging from the feeling and power she threw into the rendition of this sweet old song, she must have been a Kentuckian. At any rate, it made me so homesick that I decided when the boat arrived at Louisville to remain there. Thus ended my experiences on the river.

On my first visit to Louisville, I lived with Mrs. Matilda Gibson, an old friend of the family from Bardstown; she was a most estimable woman and very kind to me. To a lonely lad away from home the friendship of a kind, motherly woman is of inestimable value and I have never forgotten the homelike days at Mrs. Gibson's. Afterwards I made my home with my eldest brother, Henry, who had lived in the city about ten years and who had recently married. While here I continued my education by employing private teachers, first Prof. Rebeault and then Prof. Hayes, both teachers of the white High School, who instructed me in Physics, Rhetoric, and an English course in Divinity.

In 1876 I again secured employment at the Willard Hotel. I had not been there long before Mr. Ives, the proprietor of the Bates Hotel, of Indianapolis, came to Louisville to hire a crew of waiters for his house at a considerable advance of wages. My brother Isaac and I joined the crew. Indianapolis proved a blessing to us both. We enjoyed the delightful associations of interesting and intelligent persons through whom we gained an entrance into the various phases of community life. It was here that we both united with the leading fraternal societies, the Masons, Odd Fellows and the United Brethren of Friendship, in the last named of which I became a national officer.

It was my good fortune while employed at the Bates House in Indianapolis to meet Miss Katie Knox, a native of Louisville, who afterwards became my wife. A few months prior to this time she had moved to Indianapolis with her mother and eldest sister. She was an extremely modest

YOUTHFUL DAYS

young woman, well trained and of lovable personality. Her parents, Louis and Kittie Knox, were old residents of Louisville and highly respected. We were married by Rev. D. P. Seaton, D.D., August 28, 1877. Five children were the fruit of this happy marriage: William Henry Louis, born at Corydon, Ky., July 11, 1879; Mary Elizabeth, born at Louisville, February 23, 1882, who died in infancy; Alexander Ezekiel, born at San Francisco, Cal., April 1, 1885; Lord Wellington, born at Jersey City, N. J., August 4, 1891.

Mrs. Katie Walters was especially fitted to be a minister's wife. For nineteen years she labored at my side, giving me comfort, inspiration, rejoicing in my successes, and sorrowing with me in my failures. She was an eminently pious woman, an indulgent mother and a loyal friend. She died in Jersey City, December 22, 1896.

III

EARLY RELIGIOUS IMPRESSIONS, CONVERSION, ETC.

> "We take with solemn thankfulness
> Our burden up, nor ask it less;
> And count it joy that even we
> May suffer, serve or wit for Thee."
> —WHITTIER.

I RECEIVED my first religious awakening, when but a small boy, on reading the Book of Revelation. I felt sure that I was doomed to be lost. About this time, dreaming for two nights in succession of the Judgment Day and the horrors thereof, I was so frightened that I began to pray in earnest.

Rev. Yarmouth Carr was the pastor of the A. M. E. Zion Church at Bardstown at this time. I revealed to him my agitated state of mind, and was admonished by him to go to the mourners' bench, which I did; he also gave me a religious book, the name of which I cannot remember. Soon afterwards I made a profession of religion and joined the A. M. E. Zion Church; this was in 1870. I have always made it a point when taking up my residence in any city, especially if I intended to remain any length of time, to join a church, and

RELIGIOUS IMPRESSIONS 35

the Zion Church if one could be found. When I first went to Indianapolis, there was no Zion Church there, and so I joined the Vermont Street A. M. E. Church, under the pastorate of the Rev. D. P. Seaton.

A few months afterwards I assisted the Rev. Anthony Bunch to organize the A. M. E. Zion Church in Indianapolis. Prior to his coming to Indianapolis, he had been my pastor at Bardstown. He was a noted church builder.

In March, 1877, I was licensed to preach by the Quarterly Conference and pastor of this newly-organized church. On September 10, 1878, I was admitted into the Kentucky Conference of the A. M. E. Zion Church at Jones Tabernacle, Indianapolis, Ind., over which Bishop S. T. Jones presided. I was appointed from this conference to the Corydon Circuit, which consisted of Corydon and Smithmills, Kentucky. The church at Corydon was blessed with a gracious revival, the first year of my pastorate. Over fifty souls were converted and a large number added to the church.

At the Kentucky Conference, which met at St. Louis, Mo., July 3, 1879, Bishop S. T. Jones presiding, I was ordained a deacon on July 8. From this conference I was reappointed to the Corydon Circuit, and remained there two years. In connection with my other work, I was principal of the Corydon Public School. On April 7, 1881, the Kentucky Conference met at Louisville, Ky., in Jacob Street Tabernacle, Bishop S. T. Jones again presiding. I had the honor to be elected assistant secretary of this conference, and passed a most creditable examination for Elder's orders. I was appointed to the Cloverport Circuit, which consisted of Cloverport, Shawler's Chapel, Patesville, Holt's Bottom and Lick Run. There was not a church on the whole circuit, and when I reached Cloverport I was informed of the barrenness of the work. I was utterly discouraged. Remembering that I had a wife and child to support, I could not refrain from shedding tears. In that hour something seemed to say to me: "Be of good courage, up and go to work." I at once set about getting things in shape, held meetings under brush arbors, and in the school houses, and conducted special revival meetings. I bought lumber to build a church at Holt's Bottom, but ere I could put up the building, the conference met at Russellville, Ky., and I was changed from this circuit to the Fifteenth Street Church, Louisville, Ky., which was a frame building about 40 by 60 ft., and in a dilapidated condition.

The large congregation that had worshipped in this church had moved to a magnificent brick structure on Twelfth Street, between Market and Jefferson Streets. It was their intention to sell the Fifteenth Street property, and use the money to assist in paying off the debt of the Twelfth Street Church. However, they were prevented from doing so by the Conference, which refused to grant them the authority to make the sale, and because a few of the older members were not willing to leave. In all there were about twenty-five members. Notwithstanding the discouraging outlook, we took hold and were successful in improving the property and added more than a hundred to the membership.

IV

EXPERIENCES IN LOUISVILLE

> "Thou callest me to seek Thy face;—
> 'Tis all I wish to seek;
> To attend the whispers of Thy grace,
> And hear Thee inly speak."

LOUISVILLE, the metropolis of Kentucky, is one of the most beautiful and progressive cities in the South. It is situated on the south bank of the Ohio River, southwest of Cincinnati, Ohio, and has a population of 205,000. Its large mercantile houses, splendid stores, interesting municipal buildings, and aggressive business men and women give it the appearance of a prosperous city. Here are to be found some of the most renowned families of the South.

The streets are broad, regular, intersecting each other at right angles, and are beautifully shaded with trees. This is especially true of Gray Street. Its tall interlacing elms form a complete arcade. Fourth Street is Louisville's great promenade avenue. The corner of Jefferson and Fourth Streets is a famous point where the tourists from all parts of the world station themselves to view the passing throng of Kentucky's far-

FIRST SCHOOLHOUSE AND CHURCH ATTENDED BY BISHOP WALTERS

EXPERIENCES IN LOUISVILLE

famed belles. Broadway is celebrated for its width and beauty.

Louisville has a number of splendid church edifices, which would do credit to any city. Some of them are owned and completely controlled by colored people. The city maintains the separate school system, but it can be said to the credit of the broad-minded white citizens of Louisville that the colored and white schools are kept at a parity. The school buildings for colored pupils are among the largest, handsomest and best equipped in the country; well heated and lighted, with every facility for the intellectual and physical development of the students. These schools were fortunate in their early history to have at their head three of the ablest pedagogues that the race has ever produced, in the persons of Professors J. W. Maxwell of the Central High School, W. T. Payton of the Western School, W. H. Perry of the Eastern School, and later, Professors A. E. Meyzeek, Frank Williams, A. Delaney, S. B. Taylor, Daniel Lawson; Miss Lucy Duvalle, Mrs. Lelia Coleman Brown. These able instructors were efficiently and loyally supported by an excellent corps of teachers, such as Professors C. W. Houser, J. E. Simpson, Pratt Annis, James Harris, J. J. McKinley; Miss Virginia Burkes, Miss Martha Webster, Mrs. Mary L. Meade, Mrs. Mary Johnson, Miss Georgie Moore, Miss Maria Henry, Miss Eliza Davenport, Miss Belle Alexander, Miss Mary Hicks and others.

My wife, Lelia Coleman Walters, speaking of

the late Professor J. W. Maxwell, her old teacher, says: "He was unique in his position, first and ever a thorough and close student, an ideal teacher, a Christian gentleman of the sweetest and most gentle personality. Never was master more beloved by teachers and pupils than he. How well the name of master suited him. In him the student recognized the master of the subject. To go to Professor Maxwell for enlightenment on a question or subject was to have all the difficulties cleared away and to open up a beautiful vista of knowledge, so entrancing in its pursuit that the student left his presence aflame with desire for wisdom."

Socially the Afro-Americans of Louisville take first rank among the most intellectual and cultured of our land. Many of them own their own homes, and a few have elegant residences. There are a number of business enterprises operated by colored people, such as: contracting, tailoring, shoemaking, with drugstores, insurance companies and undertaking establishments.

Mr. D. W. Knight has a flourishing transfer business. Among Louisville's most prominent citizens are Revs. J. Frank, C. H. Parish, Daniel Geddie; Drs. Whedbee, Porter, Fuller, Stone and others; Mr. W. H. Steward, Mr. David Steward, Mr. and Mrs. Andrew Jackson, and Miss Minnie Rhodes, a popular trained nurse.

I feel that this chapter would be incomplete without a word concerning two of my warmest and closest friends, Mr. and Mrs. Wm. Watson;

EXPERIENCES IN LOUISVILLE

until the time of his death, Mr. Watson was one of Louisville's leading business men. He was born in this city some time in the fifties, took advantage of the early pay school system, and made his way up from the lower ranks:

"Honor and fame from no condition rise,
Act well your part, there all honor lies."

This he did.

Being intelligent, polite, obliging and honest, he won the confidence and respect of Louisville's wealthy citizens, young and old, and when reaching manhood, he determined to enter the business world for himself, he found that his early upright life had been as "bread cast upon the waters"—now bringing reward manyfold.

The greater part of Mr. Watson's life was spent in the undertaking business or directing of funerals. In addition, he conducted a general carriage business, his equipages and stock being among the finest in the city and constantly in demand by the white undertakers, of whose association he was a member. He could well be considered a pioneer in the business world of his native city, for at the time he entered business there was but one other colored firm. As to his business life, nothing but good can be said. He was successful from the beginning.

William Watson knew no difference as to treatment of his patrons. This noble man ended this life December 29, 1905. He was one who was an honor to his race, a benefactor to the community in which he lived, an upright citizen, a loving husband and a true friend and Christian. Let us reverse Shakespeare's words and say,

"The good that men do lives after them,
The evil is interred with their bones."

Mr. Watson's estimable wife Lavinia, who for twelve happy years shared his successes, and made light his dark days of adversity by her sympathy, is a woman of rare business ability—she is cultured, intelligent and generous to a fault.

"A faithful wife
Becomes the truest and the tenderest friend,
The balm of comfort and the sound of joy;
Through every various turn of life the same."

Nothing could better represent or express the relation between this couple. In his many beautiful acts of charity he was guided by this kind and loving woman.

Prior to Mr. Watson's death his interesting and beautiful home was noted far and wide for its lavish hospitality; while Mr. Watson was of a modest and very retiring disposition, yet he wanted his wife to slight no friend that called.

The "latch string" hung out, and true Kentucky hospitality was ever dispensed to all and at all times by Mrs. Lavinia Watson.

But it is not as a dispenser of hospitality that

the character of William Watson's wife shines forth in all splendor; it is as "his angel of mercy" in the last years of Mr. Watson's life, when health and strength had failed, he leaned upon her support—looked to her for the cooling draught in fever's fitful moments. The loving fidelity of this good woman to an afflicted husband was something beautiful and endeared her to the many friends he left behind.

Mrs. Watson is at the head of the business left by her husband, and is conducting the same upon the high plane of service and integrity established by its founder. Mrs. Watson has since become the wife of Mr. J. B. Cooper, and they are jointly conducting the business quite successfully,

V

AT THE GOLDEN GATE

<blockquote>
At the Golden Gate I stand
Amazed at the beauties of the land!
</blockquote>

IN the early part of May, 1883, in company with Elders E. H. Curry, J. B. Johnson, I took a trip from Louisville, Kentucky, to St. Louis, Missouri. While on the train my eyes chanced to fall on the following passage of scripture: "I will make thee unto this people a fenced brazen wall, and they shall fight against thee, but they shall not prevail against thee; for I am with thee to save thee, and to deliver thee, saith the Lord. And I will deliver thee out of the hand of the wicked, and will redeem thee out of the hand of the terrible." Jeremiah 15:20-21.

This promise to Jeremiah struck me forcibly, indeed, I could not help but apply it to myself, so impressed was I with these words, until I felt impelled to call the attention of the Reverends Curry and Johnson to them.

On reaching St. Louis, I met Bishop J. W. Hood, D.D.; it was my first meeting with the good bishop. On the same evening, we attended class-

AT THE GOLDEN GATE 45

meeting at Washington Chapel, at which place I spoke. When I took my seat, the bishop asked me if I used tobacco in any way. I answered no. He then told me that while I was speaking, he was impressed to appoint me pastor of the Stockton Street Church, San Francisco, California; but, said he, they do not want any one who uses tobacco in any form. Until he had spoken I did not know that the pulpit was vacant. I at once realized the significance of the promise given me on the train: "That I will make thee unto this people a fenced brazen wall," etc. With this promise before me I consented to go.

I arrived in San Francisco, July 5, 1883, found the church in a good financial condition, but very low spiritually. This did not discourage me. I had a large church which originally cost $80,000; 80 ft. by 120 ft. San Francisco is a magnificent city, seated like ancient Rome on seven hills. With plenty of money to draw upon, and the promise of God that I would succeed, I took hold with a vim. The first thing I did was to consecrate myself to God, and plead earnestly to be given power to win souls. My sister, who visited me about a year after my arrival here, was converted in one of our meetings. Sixty were added to the church.

October 7, 1883, I dedicated our new church at Portland, Ore. I also visited San José, Los Angeles, and other points on the coast, as presiding elder, giving encouragement to the pastors, and in every way within my power strengthening the work. The three years I spent in San Francisco were the happiest and most devoted of all my life. I can truthfully say that I lived a sanctified life; I did not possess adamic nor angelic perfection, but perfect love.

Mrs. Julia Foote, the noted evangelist, rendered me most valuable services while on the coast; indeed, from 1884 until the year she died, 1901, she made my house her home. All the members of my family were greatly indebted to this godly woman for her gracious influence in the home. She was a great preacher, an uncompromising advocate of holiness, and who practiced the gospel she preached.

May, 1884, I represented the California Conference at the General Conference, held in Mother Zion, Tenth and Bleecker Streets, New York City. It was my first appearance in a General Conference. I had the honor to be elected first assistant secretary, and was a member of the following committees: Revision, Education, Districting the Bishops, Devotion and Auditing. It was a memorable session. It was at this session that Bishop Hillery was deposed from the bishopric.

I was greatly aided in my expenses by Mrs. Mary E. Pleasants (colored), of San Francisco. She contributed two hundred dollars, in gold, toward my fare. While absent from the coast, I visited the principal cities of the East, West, North and South. Among the places visited was my old home, Bardstown, Kentucky. I was pres-

AT THE GOLDEN GATE 47

ent at the National Convention, held in Chicago, Ill., which met June 3, 1884, at which convention the Hon. James G. Blaine was nominated for the presidency. It was my first visit to a National Convention. I was especially delighted with the election of the Hon. J. R. Lynch of Mississippi as temporary chairman, and his felicitous speech on taking the chair. I returned to my work, much improved in health.

Tuesday, Sept. 9, 1884, I was awakened about six o'clock in the morning with a wonderful weight of glory; it seemed to me that heaven had entered anew into my soul, and all the day long it was "Glory, Glory, Glory." A splendid revival followed this fresh baptism. For three months, with the exception of one day, our church had been praying for the baptism of power, and not without success.

December 31, 1884, was a great night in old Stockton Street Church; more than twelve hundred people were present. God greatly blessed the following text to the salvation of many: "But of him are ye in Christ Jesus, who of God is made unto us, wisdom and righteousness and redemption." I Cor. 1:30.

The year had been an unusually happy one to me. January 1, 1885, was with me a day of much peace and great rejoicing.

August 20, 1885, my wife and three children left California for the East to visit her mother, who was very ill, and who died November 30, 1885; my little son Julien died in Louisville, December

22, 1885. My wife did not return to the coast any more. It was not my privilege to see her again until the following March.

October 19, 1885, Dr. J. C. Price, President of Livingstone College, visited the coast through an urgent invitation, which I had sent him. Plans had been inaugurated for a financial campaign, and during the three months which he was with me, he collected $8500, which enabled him to build Hopkins and Stanford Halls. Dr. Price made a wonderful impression upon the people along the coast. He spoke in the largest churches, theatres and halls in the city, and was always greeted with an immense audience. His able addresses were listened to with rapt attention, and applauded to the very echo. He was given headquarters at the Y. M. C. A. Rooms, and Mr. McCoy, secretary, rendered him valuable assistance. No colored man who has visited the coast has ever received the honors given to Dr. Price. He electrified the entire coast, and in the common parlance of the boys on the street, "he set the place on fire and left it burning."

I succeeded in paying off the large mortgage debt during my three years pastorate there.

Among the prominent families of the church were: George Dennis, Senior, who had a very intelligent family; Ezekiel Cooper, Samuel Freeman, James Hargrove, Prof. Haman, Mrs. Joseph Campbell, Richard Ricker and others.

Before closing this chapter, I do not think it is out of place to relate here an incident, which

AT THE GOLDEN GATE

occurred while I was pastor of the Stockton Street Church, San Francisco, California.

One Saturday night, while upon my knees, making preparation for the Sabbath service, I had what I suppose some people would call a vision. It seemed that some one in spirit form entered the room, proffering to me an exalted office; I realized that it was the bishopric of the church. I shrank from the responsibility and said, I am not sufficiently prepared to accept such a sacred office. Assurance was given me of divine help and constant guidance and assistance of the Holy Spirit. I thereupon burst into tears, and said: "Thy will be done." Upon my acquiescence, a peculiar peace came to my soul, and from that hour to the day of my election, eight years afterward, I felt confident that I would be a bishop in our church.

VI

CHATTANOOGA AND KNOXVILLE

> "Nor doubt that golden chords
> Of good works, mingling with the visions, raise
> The soul to purer worlds."
> —WORDSWORTH.

ON March 1, 1886, I left San Francisco, for Chattanooga, Tenn., where I had been appointed by Bishop J. W. Hood. I arrived at Chattanooga, March 12, 1886, and was given a most cordial welcome by the members and friends of the church. On March 14th, the first Sunday in my new charge, I began a revival, which lasted two weeks. About forty professed religion and united with the church. I found the people to be loyal and loving, hence was much pleased with the church.

A great flood visited the city during the spring of 1886, and by it six thousand people were made homeless. My arduous labors about this time caused me to break down physically and for six months I was unable to occupy my pulpit; the most of the time being spent at Rhea's Springs, Tenn. With this exception I had a most successful year at this point, but owing to my continued ill health, I was changed to Knoxville, Tenn.

CHATTANOOGA AND KNOXVILLE 51

The Logan Temple Church had just been finished by Dr. A. J. Warner, but owing to some misunderstanding between himself and the trustees there had been a split in the church, and when I reached Knoxville, on November 12, I found the majority of the members worshipping in a hall with Rev. Warner as their pastor, and a small minority, with the trustees, still occupied the church. I set about to reconcile the factions and finally succeeded in getting the members back into the church, while the Rev. Dr. Warner accepted a transfer to the West Alabama Conference and took charge of what is now known as Big Zion at Mobile, Ala.

I remained two years at Knoxville and had a splendid revival and succeeded in reorganizing the church, and so arranged the financial affairs as to make the church safe to the connection.

I became secretary and steward of the Tennessee Conference, and at the Conference which was held at Rogersville, October 25, 1886, over which Bishop T. H. Lomax presided, I was elected delegate to the General Conference which met at Newbern, N. C. It was a memorable session of the General Conference. It was the battlefield where ultra conservatism died in our church. The young progressive element, led by Dr. J. C. Price, achieved a signal victory over the old régime; it was the beginning of the phenomenal success of the A. M. E. Zion connection. At the close of this General Conference I was transferred from the Tennessee to the New York Conference, and stationed at Mother Zion, New York City. I arrived June 13th, and was given a most cordial welcome and reception by the members and friends.

I was soon comfortably situated with my family at No. 66 Grove Street, which for a number of years had been the parsonage of Mother Zion.

VII

THE GREAT METROPOLIS

> "Yet God is present in this place,
> Veil'd in serener majesty;
> So full of glory, truth and grace,
> That faith alone such light can see."

I HAD visited this Metropolitan City in the spring of 1884, a while before and during the session of our General Conference, which met in Mother Zion in May of the same year. I was amazed at its inhabitants, astonished at the enterprise and aggressiveness of its business men and delighted with its beautiful and immense park. I saw for the first time an elevated railroad, transporting to and fro a half million people a day.

A visit to the Stock Exchange in Wall Street, where I heard the mad roar of the speculators, convinced me that these frenzied money lovers had been correctly dubbed the "bulls and bears."

At the head of Wall Street is great Trinity (Protestant Episcopal Church), where it was my good fortune and pleasure to hear the renowned Boston preacher, the late Phillips Brooks, whose influence was world wide. Not far away from Trinity, on Broadway, is old St. Paul. It was in this church, 1789, that George Washington took the oath of office as President of the United States. Within a stone's throw of St. Paul's Church is the City Hall, Post-office, the famous Brooklyn Bridge, and the great Metropolitan daily papers, *Tribune, Herald, Journal, World, Press, Times, Sun, Post, Mail and Express,* and a great number of magazines and other periodicals. From this centre radiates the greatest intellectual and financial influence of the nation; indeed, from this centre the financial world is controlled.

It was to this mammoth city with its many churches and its multitudinous interests that I had been sent to touch and help develop its spiritual life as best I could. I considered myself fortunate in being appointed at the age of thirty, to look after the affairs of Mother Zion.

The church was a commodious brick edifice, which could accommodate two thousand people, when filled to its utmost capacity. The organization was formed in 1796 and incorporated in 1801. Some of the most distinguished men of our connection had pastored this church. Delighted with the charge and finding the people ready to work, I took hold to succeed or die in the attempt. The church had lost a large part of its congregation, and was at a low ebb spiritually. I saw at once that the first thing to do was to get the people back into the church, and I considered that the best way to do this was to have a revival of religion, and to that end I preached for six months,

THE HOUSE IN WHICH MRS. LELIA WALTERS WAS BORN

THE GREAT METROPOLIS 55

preached on the law, until one night, going home from church, my wife said to me, that she thought that I had given them law enough, and that they were sore and needed some gospel of love. I considered her a pretty good judge; hence on January 1, 1889, I opened a revival by preaching from John 3:16: "For God so loved the world that he gave his only begotten Son, that whosoever believeth in him should not perish, but have everlasting life."

The meetings continued about three months; over three hundred joined the church and more than that number were converted. It was a real refreshing from the presence of the Lord. I was assisted in the meetings by the Rev. Mrs. Foote, the renowned woman evangelist; Rev. James M. Butler, son of the late William F. Butler, who had been a popular minister of the church, some years prior to my pastorate there; Deacon William Phillips, with a strong array of enthusiastic Christian workers, called the "battle boys and girls"; George and Peter Washington, James Chase, Philip Williams, James Nixon, Edward Williams, William Fisher, E. V. C. Eto, John Pulley, Philip Richardson, Alfred Abrams, William Fisher, David Landrine, Isaac Majors, Anderson Burrell, Jacob Hutchins, Fisher Sampson, N. F. Allen (white).

Among the women were Jane Thomas, Hannah Wardell, Charlotte Fisher, Elizabeth Purnell, Fanny Van Brunk, Alexzenio Thomas, Ruby Johnson, Ida Dawson, Dinah Myers, Jerusha

Vogelsong; Mothers Mosley, Johnson, Thomas, Vincent and others. I was also supported by a strong board of trustees in the persons of Richard Harris, president; E. V. C. Eto, secretary, who had been superintendent of the A. M. E. Zion Sunday School for twenty-five years; Jacob James, Brother Troatman, treasurer. Charles Randall, Jacob Wells, John Palmer, Jacob Hutchins and John Jackson.

It was during the first year of my pastorate at Mother Zion that I was appointed by the Board of Bishops to represent the Zion Connection at the World's Sunday School Convention, which was to be held July 6, 1889, at London, England. Besides this appointment, I was also elected as one of the delegates of the Sunday School Union of the State of New York.

VIII

EUROPE

> "The new sight, the new wondrous sight!
> The waters round me turbulent,
> The skies impassive o'er me!"
> —Mrs. Browning.

ON the 19th of June, 1889, in company with Drs. D. P. Seaton, of the A. M. E. Church; Walter Brooks, J. D. Olden, of the Baptist Church; George Moore, of the Congregational Church; C. H. Phillips, of the C. M. E. Church, and over three hundred Sunday school workers (white) from all parts of America, we sailed on the steamship *Bothnia*, Cunard Line, for Liverpool, England, to attend the World's Sunday School Convention, which met in London, July 6th of the same year.

The first thing of interest to me, which occurred on board after our period of sea-sickness, was a "set-back" given by the steward to a young Southerner who was assigned a seat next to mine, in the dinner hall. I happened to be seated at the table before he came in; when he arrived and saw me sitting there, he remarked to the steward that he was not going to eat by the side of a "Nigger." The steward being English, did not seem to comprehend what he meant by that statement and hence paid very little attention to him. He withdrew without his meal. At the next meal I chanced to arrive at the table again in advance of him; when he reached his seat he reddened in the face and again told the steward that he would not sit by me, and demanded another seat. The steward's face reddened, and pointing his finger at the seat, he said to him: "Young man, you will take your meals at that seat, or you will not eat on board this ship." I said to myself, "Thank God for English fair play!" I was not treated better by any one on board the ship after this than I was by that young man who at first refused to eat by my side.

What some of the white people of this country need is for those in authority to give them to understand that they are going to accord to every man his rights, whether he be white or black. Let those who administer the laws impress upon the people that they must obey the laws, and all this trouble which we are having because of race prejudice, etc., will soon pass away.

After ten days' sail, we arrived at Liverpool on a Sunday morning. We were given a reception by the Sunday School Union of Liverpool on Sunday evening, at the Young Men's Christian Association Rooms, a very spacious building of that city. The hall was packed to its utmost capacity. Strange to say, the colored brethren were left off the program. The speaking had not been going on long, before a voice was heard saying: "We want to hear the colored men; let one of the colored delegates speak." Mr. B. F. Jacobs of Chicago, Chairman of the delegation, called several of us to the platform.

The colored delegates were given a regular ovation. The enthusiasm reached its highest bounds, when one of the delegates remarked that he was glad to be on English soil, because there was a time when the courageous, liberty-loving Negro, fleeing from the wrath of his master, pursued by the bloodhounds, sought English soil, and reaching it found himself under the protection of the Union Jack, when he could turn and grin in his master's face and say: "Touch me if you dare!" In conclusion he said: "In those dark days when we had but few friends in our own country, you stood ready at all times to befriend us. We can never forget your kindness."

Our welcome was so cordial, that when Dr. Wharton, of Baltimore, Md., rose to speak and was accorded a rather cold reception, he said: "For one time in my life, I wish I was a colored man." We had scored.

We left Liverpool the next morning and stopped at Bedford, the home of John Bunyan. It was in this city he was incarcerated in prison for twelve years; here he wrote his immortal work, "Pilgrim's Progress."

On reaching London, the delegation was tendered a reception at the Mansion House, by the Lord Mayor of London. Again the colored delegates were left off the program; we thought surely there was no way for us to receive any recognition whatever. But when the speaking was all over, and the Mayoress on the arm of the Lord Mayor, came down from the throne, to go into the luncheon room, she stopped the royal procession and seeing the colored delegates standing near the door, she said to one of her attendants: "Invite those colored gentlemen here." On invitation we stepped forward. She asked our names, wished us a pleasant stay in London and a successful session; and then requested us to form an escort to conduct them into the luncheon room. We did so, to the great consternation of our white brethren.

At Exeter Hall a few nights after this the colored delegates made such an impression that several of them were invited to make their homes with some of the prominent citizens of London. Your humble servant happened to be one of the favored ones. I was taken from my hotel, bag and baggage, to the elegant residence of one of the Assemblymen of London, Mr. Samuel Cole. I had not been at his residence long before I found that I was in the midst of the élite of London. Indeed, as the vulgar phrase puts it, I was "in the swim."

The next morning, after I was domiciled, the maid rapped at the door and asked for my shoes. I understood this and put them on the outside. Soon after this I was invited down to breakfast. I donned my morning robe and went below; was heartily greeted by the members of the family and took breakfast in royal style, as if I had been used to it all my life.

I returned to my room and had not been there long when a gentle tap came at the door; a maid entered and said to my surprise, "Sir, your carriage is ready." I could not imagine for the life of me what it meant. Of course I did not wish to have it known that I was not accustomed to all the luxuries of life and acquainted with all the rules of etiquette. I therefore replied, "All right."

Upon this the thought occurred to me to step to the window; on doing so I saw the carriage at the door with footman and driver; I surmised I was to go out for a morning drive. I put on my things as quickly as possible, and on reaching the lower hall was met by my host and hostess. With all the dignity of a gentleman of leisure and luxury, I announced my readiness. This was repeated every morning and afternoon for two weeks.

One Saturday afternoon Mr. Cole informed me that he would be busy on the Sabbath and wished to know if I would accompany Mrs. Cole and a lady friend from Scotland to church. I told them I would do so. A thought occurred to me (I know not whence it came) to take advantage of the occasion to have some fun with our white American brethren and let them see how a colored man was respected and honored in England. The whole delegation had been invited to worship at Mr. Spurgeon's church; the invitation had been accepted and I knew they were all likely to be present. I went to a gents' furnishing store and instructed the salesman to fit my hand with a pair of kid gloves of the latest, and told him not to regard the cost, as I wanted a neat fit. He seemed to appreciate the situation, and although he did not know what it was, he thought there was "something up." Believe me, when I tell you he gave me the neatest fit I ever had in my life; I had not cared for gloves very much, heretofore, but I was especially anxious to have the best in the market on this occasion. I had purchased a new suit before leaving home for the convention. With my new suit, kid gloves and low quartered shoes, I was prepared to escort the ladies to church.

I could not sleep well on Saturday night for thinking of my approaching triumph. I arose early Sunday morning and long before the maid came to announce that the carriage was in waiting, I was ready. Finally the hour arrived, I appeared in the hall arrayed in an "up-to-date" outfit, and informed the ladies that I was at their service.

After I had assisted them into the carriage, I said to the footman (putting something in his hand), "If you see a great many carriages in front of the church when we arrive, you saunter about until the way is cleared." I knew the white delegates from America would be waiting in front of the church, as strangers had to wait at Mr. Spurgeon's church till the pew holders arrived, or at least until half past ten o'clock. If the pew

EUROPE

holders were not in their seats by that time, anyone could take their places.

The driver and the footman seemed to sympathize with me. There happened to be a number of carriages about the entrance; the driver sauntered about till the way was cleared and then drove up to the curb. The footman opened the door; I stepped out and with my neatly-gloved hand assisted Mrs. Cole and her friend to alight.

With all the grace imaginable, and in full view of the assembled multitude, who stood gazing on with amazement, I escorted the ladies into the church, much to the astonishment of my deeply prejudiced Southern brethren. I don't know when I have gotten so much real enjoyment out of an occasion, furnished ready to hand by unreasonable prejudice.

One day when we were visiting the Zoological Gardens I burst into a fit of laughter. Mrs. Cole asked me what in the world could be the matter. I said, "Nothing." But she said, "Mr. Walters, there must be something the matter." And she pressed me so hard to tell her that I promised I would. I will tell you what it was.

I happened to reach a cage while visiting the menagerie department which contained a great big baboon, which reminded me of a story I heard in one of the Southern conferences about a man who lived on a Southern plantation by the name of Tom; his master, hearing there was a show to visit the town, said to him one day: "Tom, if you will be a good boy, I will let you go to the show." Tom took him up, did his best and succeeded in keeping in favor with his master till the show came. The day arrived; Tom, with his bare feet, went to town and waited for his master to come, and pay his way into the show. Finally his master came and Tom went in; he looked at the tigers, lions, bears, etc.

At last he came to a cage and saw something in it which he thought was an old-time darkey. Seeing him chained, he sympathized with him and said: "What have you done that the white folks got you tied up like this? They had me tied up like this once and I prayed to God and He delivered me. If you pray to God He will deliver you too." He saw the white folks looking towards him and said: "I can't talk to you any longer; I see the white folks looking and they don't allow us colored folks to stand and talk together too long. So good-bye." He reached his hands through the bars to bid his supposed ancestor farewell. It was a baboon, and he struck his hand and nearly cut it off. He aroused the whole circus by his screams and cried: "That is just what I say about my people; if you tell them anything for their own good, they will try to kill you!"

This greatly amused my friends, and I was ever and anon being reminded of the fact that if I told my people anything for their own good, I would be nearly killed for it.

The first place we visited was Westminster Abbey. It was founded in the eighth century

EUROPE

and was not completed till the thirteenth. It is in the form of an irregular cross: its length, exclusive of the chapel of Henry the Seventh, is 511 feet; width 203 feet; height 225 feet. All the British sovereigns from Edward the Confessor to Queen Victoria have been crowned in this great Abbey, and some of them have been buried there.

The next place visited was St. Paul's Cathedral. The length of this Cathedral is 510 feet; width 250 feet; from the pavement to the top of the cross on the dome is 440 feet. In it lie the remains of Lord Wellington (after whom it has been my pleasure and delight to name my youngest son), Lord Nelson, John Moore, Sir Christopher Wren, John Howard and others. This is the greatest edifice of the kind in all the British Isles.

The exterior of this building is not as imposing as our Capitol at Washington; the interior, some think, surpasses the interior of our Capitol. I hardly think so. It was by the kindness of Mr. Lincoln, who was our minister at the Court of St. James at that time, that I was permitted to enter the House of Commons and the House of Lords. After entering I had the pleasure of hearing Mr. Gladstone and also Mr. Balfour, who was then secretary for Ireland, and other distinguished statesmen of England.

While sitting there I imagined that I could see Charles I. I was present in my imagination at this great trial; I saw the witnesses as they testified against him; I heard the great Commoner (than whom there has been no greater, even Gladstone himself), Oliver Cromwell, call the liberty-loving hosts to arms. I saw them behead Charles, and then heard them proclaim Cromwell, Lord Protector. I heard the eloquence of a Burke; was present at the trial of Warren Hastings; indeed, listened to all the great intellectual battles which had been fought in those halls through the centuries.

At one time it was Walpole that I saw in control of affairs. At another time Pitt. Mine own eyes beheld Gladstone with the reins in his hands.

From the House of Parliament we went to the Tower of London, which existed at the time of Julius Cæsar. The White Tower was erected by William the Conqueror; 8,000 soldiers are garrisoned in the Tower. Here are kept the crowned jewels of England, worth $20,000,000, and which are guarded continually by some of the best trained soldiers of the Queen.

Buckingham Palace, the city residence of the Queen, was next visited. On the day I visited the palace I had the extreme pleasure of seeing the Shah of Persia, who was on a visit to England; also Prince Albert and his royal family in the royal carriages. Buckingham Palace is a magnificent structure. I did not see the Queen at this time, but later, at Windsor Castle.

Prince Albert Memorial, the most splendid monument of modern time, was next visited. At the corners are marble groups representing Asia, Europe, Africa and America; in the centre is a life-sized figure of Albert. One hundred and sixty-nine life-sized portraits of England's distinguished poets, orators, etc., adorn this magnificent Memorial.

We next turned our steps to the British Museum, the finest of the kind in the world. It contains some of the oldest and most valuable manuscripts extant; in it are many rare paintings and other works of art.

After visiting some other places of interest and being entertained by the Count and Countess of Aberdeen, I left for the Continent. The first place I visited there was Antwerp, in Belgium. The Cathedral here is the most interesting thing in the city. It was eighty years in building. Length 500 feet; width 250 feet; height 405 feet.

Brussels was next visited. It is Paris on a small scale; the streets are broad and well laid out. The King's palace is here. The House of Parliament is a splendid specimen of architecture. After spending some time at Brussels enjoying the refreshing breezes I left for Cologne, Germany. This is one of the oldest cities in Germany; here I saw the women in the market places with white handkerchiefs on their heads, wooden shoes, etc. These old German women look fat and lusty.

The great Cathedral of Cologne, which is the finest in Northern Europe, was commenced in the thirteenth century, and finished in the nineteenth. The cost was nearly $4,000,000. Its length is 511 feet; height of the Tower 511 feet; width 231 feet.

Seven hundred and twenty-six stone statues adorn it. The choir and windows are superb. The columns and paintings are grand and imposing beyond description. It is useless for me to attempt to describe them. But this was not the church I was most interested in at Cologne; it was the church of St. Ursala. This church is lined with the bones of 6,000 martyrs of the Theban legion, which were slain here in the year 286, by order of the Emperor Diocletian. It is one of the finest churches in Cologne.

The next place I visited in Germany was Strasburg, the city containing the celebrated astronomical clock. From Strasburg I went to Worms. Here is where Martin Luther met the Diet, so famous in Ecclesiastical history. After visiting several other points in Germany, I left for Switzerland. The first place of interest in that country at which I stopped was Lucerne, situated on a small lake of the same name. Geneva was also visited. There are many renowned places of interest in this renowned city.

Leaving Switzerland, my next point was Italy. The first city which I visited in Italy was Milan, where is one of the finest Cathedrals in Europe. From Milan I journeyed to Venice, the City in the Sea. Not liking Venice, I left on the next train; left my baggage behind, and did not obtain it again for a month.

I arrived next at Florence which is one of the most beautiful cities in Italy. From Florence I went to Rome. Rome is called the "Eternal City," the once Mistress of the world! the home of Julius Cæsar, Pompey and Cicero. Here I visited the Old Forum, the Coliseum, passing the magnificent Arch of Titus. I also visited St. Peter's, the largest church edifice in the world. Naples was my next destination. Near this city is Mount Vesuvius, 3937 feet above the sea.

IX

EGYPT AND THE HOLY LAND

They that go down to the sea in ships, that do business in great waters; these see the works of the Lord, and his wonders in the deep.—*Old Testament, Psalm* cvii. 23.

AT Naples I took ship for Alexandria, in Egypt. When I went upon the steamer, *Ortegia,* the chief steward was not on board; the second steward did not seem to understand English, and did not seem to know much about the ship. He put me in a very fine stateroom. Indeed, it was a bridal apartment, all beautifully upholstered. I thought it was just the place to take my goods out of my valise and set up housekeeping in good shape, since it would take us five days to cross. I had no more than finished, when the chief steward arrived. He could not speak English, and I could not speak Italian, but by gesticulation, etc., he tried to tell me that I was in the wrong place. I endeavored to make him understand by gesticulation that I did not comprehend his meaning. Finally I manufactured a language of my own, and in slow

EGYPT AND THE HOLY LAND 71

measured accents, looking him square in the face, I said: "Omfra shockto medo frala!" Don't ask me what I meant by that, as I could not tell you for the life of me. He looked at me in astonishment, as much as to say: "Why, what language do you speak, anyhow?" I took advantage of his ignorance to impress him with the fact that he had outraged my dignity, and with all the vehemence and rapidity possible I repeated the words: "Omfra shockto medo frala!"

The steward left me hastily and never returned. Believe me when I tell you I occupied the apartment unmolested clear across the Mediterranean Sea. I would see them as I went to and fro from my meals peeping from behind the smokestacks at me, wondering from what part of India the Prince came. For I learned afterwards that they believed me to be a Prince from India.

Finally, after five days' sail, I reached Alexandria and put up at the Hotel Abbot. Alexandria is quite a modern city in appearance. Here we come in contact with oriental life; long flowing robes, beautifully embroidered turbans, wide breeches, etc. I never heard such a racket in all my life as greeted me when the ship dropped anchor.

One sees a great many marks of the bombardment of July, 1882. The first sight of interest is Pompey's Pillar, which stands on the elevation and is of polished red granite, 100 feet high. The Mohammedan Cemetery is very near Pompey's Pillar. Alexandria was named in honor of the great Macedon General. Here Cleopatra lived and exercised her magic arts upon Cæsar and Marc Antony. Here the Arian heresy first originated, and it was once one of the famous Bishoprics of the world.

From Alexandria we travelled to Cairo, which is situated on the River Nile. This is the river in which Moses was placed in the basket of bulrushes. The streets are narrow and anything but clean. The wonderful pyramids which have stood for the centuries are within eight miles of this city. The bazaars are one of its chief attractions. Long lines of camels, piloted by donkeys, can be seen at any time on entering the city.

Imagine you see your bishop with a linen duster on and a plug hat, riding a little donkey, four feet high, to the great amusement of the bystanders. I asked the guide at what were all the people laughing; was it because I was a colored man? He said, "No, there are plenty people your color here." I asked him if it was my height. He said, "No, there are fine specimens of height in Cairo." I said, "Well, what is it then?" He replied, "Why, these people never saw any one here with a hat on like yours, especially on a donkey." I must confess it was a ludicrous sight.

The Citadel, or El Kalah, is said to occupy the site of the Acropolis; and the ancient Bablioum is built on the flank of a hill overlooking the town. The gate is in the form of an elliptical arch. Here the slaughter of the Memlocks took place in 1811; only one escaped out of 450; they were decoyed

MRS. LELIA WALTERS

in this edifice and murdered. It is one of the finest sights of the town.

The Palace of the Khedive presents nothing worthy of admiration. The Mosque of Mohammed Ali, erected in 1829, although built of costly material, is less interesting than the Mosque of Cairo. Its ceiling is a vast cupola surrounded by four demi-cupolas and four small domes at the corners. The whole of the interior is lined with oriental alabaster, except the upper part of the columns, which are painted to imitate that material. On the left of the entry, a golden grill encloses the tomb of Mohammed Ali, with lamps perpetually burning. From above the pavilion there is a splendid view of Cairo and lower Egypt, which some have said to be the finest view in the world. The Museum was next visited and is one of the most valuable in existence. Here we saw some ancient mummies, well preserved. The pyramids next claimed our attention. The largest one is 732 feet at the base line; perpendicular height 460 feet. The stones are from four to six feet long, and from two to four feet thick. The other pyramids are smaller.

It was under this pyramid that Napoleon said upon one occasion just before a battle: "Do your duty well to-day, for forty centuries look down from the top of yonder pyramid to see that you acquit yourselves like men."

The celebrated sphinx is near by. It is 140 feet in length; the paws 50 feet long, are built of hewn stone; the head is carved out of the solid rock and measures 30 feet from the brow to the chin, and 14 feet across. These monuments tell of the civilization of the past.

From Cairo we returned to Alexandria and took ship for Joppa. After two days' sail we landed at the port. It was here that Jonah shipped for Tarshish when commanded by the Lord to go to Nineveh, and subsequently had trouble with the whale. Here the timbers were landed which had been cut in the mountains of Lebanon to build Solomon's Temple. In this city Peter, while in a trance upon the housetop, beheld a sheet let down from heaven containing all manner of four-footed beasts of the earth, and creeping things, and fowls of the air; and there came to him a voice saying: "Arise, Peter, kill and eat." And Peter said: "Not so, Lord, for I have never eaten anything that is common or unclean." The voice spoke unto him again, the second time: "What God hath cleansed, that call not thou common." This convinced Peter.

Here Dorcas was raised to life. Here I slept on a housetop, in imitation of what Peter had done. The city is built on the side of a hill. The most of the houses are stone, with earthen floors and flat roofs in the old oriental style. There are some beautiful lemon groves about Joppa. The bazaars are very good, but not as fine as in other cities.

After visiting other places of interest in Joppa we left for Jerusalem, which is about thirty-five miles distant. The first place of note on leaving

Joppa is the Plain of Sharon, which extends from Jaffa to Cesarea. This is the Plain in which the lilies grew of which Jesus spoke. The next place is Ramleh, a village of four or five thousand inhabitants. There is a great tower near the town, and from this tower can be obtained a fine view of the Plain of Sharon, as far down as Askalon, and as far up as Mount Carmel.

Next comes the Valley of Ajalon. This valley was made famous by the battle which Joshua had with the kings. He prayed that the sun might stand still over Gibeon and the moon be stayed in the Valley of Ajalon, until he obtained the victory over his enemies.

From here we entered Koloneih; along by it runs the ravine out of which David gathered the stones with which to slay Goliath.

I imagined I could see him as he left the armies of Saul and descended the valley with God in his view, trusting in Him for help. We turned our steps next toward Emmaus, which is on a descent just before you come in sight of Jerusalem. This is the village where Christ went with His disciples on the day of the Resurrection, and reasoned with them by the way; and when He had left them they said: "Did not our hearts burn within us as He talked with us?"

A short while after leaving here we came in sight of Jerusalem. We entered on the western side, along which runs the Valley of Gihon. We entered through the Jaffa Gate; near this gate stands the old tower of David. We passed down

David Street, which is very narrow, not more than eight or ten feet wide. Camels and donkeys and the bazaars are all crowded in and along this street. We passed down into Christian Street, and before long reached the church of the Holy Sepulchre.

This is a large and spacious building containing a great many chapels. The Greeks, Latins, Armenians, Copts, Abyssinians, all have chapels under this roof. The first object shown us was the Stone of Unction. When the body of Jesus was taken down from the cross, it was laid upon the Stone for anointing. Lamps hang over and surround the stone. Under the dome, in the centre of the church, is the Holy Sepulchre; it lies within a small chapel, 26 by 18 feet, and built of marble. The hole of the Sepulchre is round, it being cut in the side of the rock. The Sepulchre, itself, is only six by seven feet. The vestibule of the chapel called the Angels' Chapel contains the stone which the angels rolled away from the mouth of the tomb. Just at the back of the Sepulchre is the Chapel of the Copts. North of the Sepulchre is an open court, where Jesus said to Mary, "Woman, why weepest thou"? Many are the sacred places round about and in the church of the Holy Sepulchre; notably the Hill of Calvary, the rent which was made in the stone on the day of Christ's death.

We next visited the Pool of Bethesda. There is no water in the Pool now, and excavations have well nigh destroyed its beauty. There is a little

EGYPT AND THE HOLY LAND

stream issuing from the Pool of Siloam. The Mosque of Omar is a place of great interest. It is built on Mt. Moriah, the spot where the old temple stood which was built by Solomon. The Mosque is surrounded by a wall 1601 feet long on the west; 1530 feet on the east; 1024 feet on the north, and 922 feet on the south. It is entered by eight gates on the west. The Jews' Wailing Place is at the old wall and is said to have been built by David. There are seven gates to the City of Jerusalem: the Jaffa Gate, Damascus Gate, St. Stephen's Gate, Dung Gate, Zion Gate, Golden Gate and Gate of Herod.

It is about two and a half miles around the walls; the walls are from 32 to 42 feet in height, and in some places 15 feet thick. On the east side of the city is the Valley of Jehoshaphat; on the south side is the Valley of Himmon. Just across this Valley is the Garden of Gethsemane; it was in this Garden that Christ was apprehended after His wonderful agony and prayer.

From Gethsemane we visited the Mount of Olives, called also Mt. Olivet. It is an inconsiderable ridge lying on the east side of Jerusalem, made famous by the ascent of the Master, from its peak in the heaven.

There is a minaret on the summit of the mountain from the top of which is one of the grandest views imaginable. Stretched at your feet is the Garden of Gethsemane and the city of Jerusalem; a little in the distance, looking toward the south, is the River Jordan and the Dead Sea. The top of

Mount Carmel is seen in the west, while Bethlehem lies to the southeast.

To Bethlehem, which is about six miles from Jerusalem, we next directed our way. Just before entering the city, we came to Rachel's tomb; it is without the City gate. This is where Jacob buried his beloved wife, Rachel. Soon after leaving Rachel's tomb, we entered Bethlehem, the birthplace of our blessed Saviour, and of our King David. It is a small walled town of four or five thousand inhabitants. The Church of the Nativity covers the grotto where Christ was born. Like the Holy Sepulchre at Jerusalem, it is subdivided among the Greeks, Armenians, Latins, etc. A silver star marked the spot where Christ was born. The manger stands in a low recess cut from the rock, a few feet from this star.

Other places of interest in the grotto are the chapel and tomb of St. Jerome; the well renowned for the libation which David poured out of water which had been gotten by a daring exploit by three of his mighty men, on hearing him exclaim: "O, that one would give me drink of the water of the well of Bethlehem, which is by the gate!" When it was brought he poured it out as a libation to the Lord, saying: "Be it far from me, O Lord, that I should do this. Is not this the blood of the men that went by jeopardy of their lives?" Therefore he would not drink of it.

Here the angels appeared unto the shepherds, telling them of the birth of Jesus, and sang an anthem in honor of the new born King. Here

EGYPT AND THE HOLY LAND

the wise men brought their gifts of gold, frankincense and myrrh, and laid them at the feet of the infant Sovereign. Over this city the star appeared which guided the wise men to the spot where the young child was born.

From Bethlehem we directed our course to Hebron, one of the oldest cities in the Land of Palestine, the home of Abraham and Jacob. It is in the cave of Macpelah that Abraham buried his beloved wife Sarah. It is now a Mosque, in possession of the Mohammedans. Not a great distance from Hebron is the Valley of Eschol, where the spies from the camp of Israel gathered grapes to carry back to Moses as a sample of the fruit of the land. The bunches were so large that they had to be borne on a pole between two men. I had the pleasure of eating grapes in this valley, which I considered a great privilege. From Hebron we returned to Bethlehem. The next route lay from there to Marsaba, which is a convent in the midst of grand scenery, utterly barren and desolate. It is a gigantic structure, built in terraces into a kind of amphitheatre on the side of the mountain.

From Marsaba our next point was the Dead Sea, called sometimes the Sea of Lot. It is about forty miles long, with an average breadth of nine miles, 1312 feet below the level of the Mediterranean Sea. It is fed by the Jordan and many other streams, but it has no apparent outlet. Its superfluous water is supposed to be carried off entirely by evaporation. The water is characterized by vast quantities of magnesia and soda salts.

The River of Jordan is the principal river of Palestine; it would be considered by an American as an insignificant river. It has a course of 150 miles and enters into the Dead Sea. It is the most historical river in the world; indeed, it is the history that clusters round the River Jordan which gives it its prominence.

Jericho is about an hour's ride from Jordan River. It was in this road from Jerusalem to Jericho that the traveller fell among thieves, who stripped, wounded him and left him for dead. Jericho was long celebrated for its beautiful groves and gardens, which were given to Cleopatra by Marc Antony. It is now a barren waste, no beauty nor comeliness about it. From Jerusalem to Jericho is a ride of about nine hours.

From thence we wended our way to Bethany, the home of Lazarus, Mary and Martha. It is a little city not far from Jerusalem. Our next trip was made to Nazareth, by way of Gibeah of Saul, Ramah of Benjamin, and Bethel, where Jacob saw the ladder, while sleeping with his head resting upon a stone. Jacob's well is here, where Christ held the conversation with the woman; Nebulus, or an ancient city of Shechem, between Mount Ebal and Mount Gerizim; the Plain of Esdraelon, and the Lake of Galilee.

In Nazareth, like most of the other towns of Palestine, the houses are built of stone, with flat

EGYPT AND THE HOLY LAND 81

roofs on the ancient order. Here lived Joseph and Mary with their son Jesus. Here Jesus spent his boyhood, roaming over the hills and doubtless carrying water from the famous well. The workshop of Joseph is here, where we are told Jesus, himself, labored.

The next journey was to Heifa; from Heifa to Jaffa, and from Jaffa back to Alexandria. At Alexandria we joined the family of the Khedive and other distinguished persons, and left for Naples. From Naples to Rome; from Rome to Genoa, where Columbus set sail for the New World. From Genoa to Turin, to Geneva. From Geneva we came to Paris, France.

The Exposition was in full blast in that city. We spent two weeks visiting places of interest. Paris is the finest city in the world; the streets are broad and magnificently laid off. We saw there the Arch of Triumph and the Place de la Concorde.

We also visited Versailles, at which city is the palace, built by Louis XIV. The Exposition was a magnificent affair; one of its chief attractions was the Eiffel Tower, 1000 feet high.

Other interesting places visited were the Column Vendôme; the Church of Nôtre Dame; the Hôtel Des Invalides; the Louvre, which was the city palace of the king, now an art gallery; the Tuileries or gardens of the king; the Grand Opera, one of the finest buildings in Paris.

After "doing" Paris I left for London, and remained there quite a long time, preaching in some of the finest Methodist and Congregational Churches in that city.

From England I went to Scotland, visiting Edinburgh and Glasgow.

From Scotland to Ireland, stopping at Dunkirk, Dublin, Killarney, Cork, Blarney Castle and Queenstown. At Queenstown I took the steamer *Etruria* for America, my native land. After six days' sail on this ocean liner, I found myself in New York harbor.

X

HOME AGAIN

"'Breathes there the man with soul so dead
Who never to himself hath said,
This is my own, my native land!
Whose heart hath ne'er within him burned
As home his footsteps he hath turned
From wandering on a foreign strand?''

ON my return home from my trip abroad, I at once began preparation for the complete renovation of Mother Zion. The ceiling was decorated after a model which I had seen in Germany. The cost was about $5000, and we were successful in raising every dollar of it ere the work was finished in October, 1890. In the fall of 1889, I was appointed by the Board of Bishops to succeed Rev. Jacob Thomas, as General Agent of the Book Concern. This institution had been located in the basement at 183 Bleecker Street, New York City. The first thing we did on taking charge was to move the few books and fixtures into our own church property, 353 Bleecker Street. The store was put in first class condition; new books and stationery bought, and the institution put into splendid running order. Miss Julia Hall was our first clerk, and remained with us about six months. She was succeeded by Mrs. Josephine Richardson, who remained with us a short while; she in turn was succeeded by Mrs. Emaline Bird Lawson, who remained with the department about nine years. In 1889, the Book Concern was removed from New York City to Charlotte, N. C., where it is now.

August, 1890, was made memorable by the great camp-meeting, held at Prohibition Park, Staten Island, N. Y., under the auspices of Mother Zion Church. Some of the most distinguished clergymen of the A. M. E. and A. M. E. Zion Church were present and took part. Notably among them were Rev. B. F. Lee, D.D. (now bishop of the A. M. E. Church); Bishop J. W. Hood, D.D.; Drs. J. C. Price, G. L. Blackwell, J. S. Caldwell (now bishop of the A. M. E. Zion Church), James H. Smith, J. S. Colbert and Jacob Thomas. At this glorious camp-meeting, Mrs. Emaline Bird Lawson was converted.

One of the chief features of the camp-meeting was the daily meeting for the Bible Study and Christian fellowship; friendships were made, which have remained unbroken till now.

Notwithstanding we were on this holy mount and "about our Father's business," we found time to make out a slate for the ensuing General Conference, which resulted in my election to the office of a bishop. My chief supporters were: Bishop J. W. Hood, Dr. J. C. Price, and Hon. J. C. Dancey. During the winter we were blessed with another outpouring of the Holy Ghost;

HOME AGAIN

nearly two hundred were converted. The Conference year was a most prosperous one.

ELECTED AND ORDAINED BISHOP

The General Conference, which met in John Wesley Church, Pittsburgh, Pa., May 4, 1892, was a memorable one in our history. The aggressive policies inaugurated were many and had been exceedingly beneficial to the church. It was composed of some of Zion's most brainy men.

On the twelfth day of May, it was decided by the General Conference that two additional bishops were needed. Thereupon the election ensued. Dr. I. C. Clinton and myself were elected bishops on the first ballot. An indescribable scene of enthusiasm followed on announcement of our election. We were carried about the church on the shoulders of our friends. I was not quite thirty-four years old when elected a bishop.

On May 11, the day prior to my election, I entered into the following covenant with Almighty God:

"O Lord, my Heavenly Father, I enter into this solemn covenant with Thee, should I by Thy grace be elected a bishop, I promise to love Thee fervently, and to serve Thee diligently all the days of my life. And to do all in my power to bring the ministry, over which I am appointed to preside, up to the highest standard of moral and Christian integrity."

When the assignment of the bishops was made, I received the Seventh Episcopal District, which comprised the following conferences: Kentucky, Missouri, Arkansas, California, West Tennessee, Mississippi and Oregon Conferences.

I was especially pleased to have the Kentucky Conference (my old home) placed in my district. Fourteen years prior to this time I had been admitted into its ranks at Indianapolis, Ind., and I was now delighted with the thought that I was to return as its Presiding Bishop.

The first session over which I presided met at Louisville, Ky., September, 1892. The brethren, many of whom knew me when I was but a lad, and others who were my schoolmates, gave me a royal welcome.

My stay among them was pleasant and profitable, at least to me and I think beneficial to the work. To my great delight the California Conference was added to my district. I had served as pastor and presiding elder in the said conference. The ministers and friends extended to me a warm and appreciative welcome. I was successful in adding several churches to the district and made large increases in the General Fund and other connectional claims.

At the Pittsburg General Conference, arrangements were made for the celebration of the 100th Anniversary of the organization of the African Methodist Episcopal Church. The following resolution was introduced by me and received a unanimous vote of the General Conference:

HOME AGAIN

"In view of the fact that the Zion Connection is approaching the period of a 100th Anniversary and it is in keeping with the spirit of the church in some becoming way to observe such anniversary, we therefore recommend that a centennial celebration be held in the leading church of each Annual Conference District. It shall be under the management of the bishop and the members of the several annual conferences. The net proceeds shall be divided between the church and the centennial fund.

"Be it further resolved that the General Celebration be held in Mother Zion Church, New York City, in September, 1896.

"Be it further resolved that a committee be appointed to make arrangements for the said anniversary. The following were appointed:

"Bishops J. W. Hood, C. C. Petty, C. R. Harris, T. H. Lomax, I. C. Clinton and A. Walters.

"Revs. G. W. Clinton, W. Howard Day, R. H. G. Dyson, J. W. Alstork, B. F. Wheeler, H. W. Smith, W. H. Chambers, Thomas Darley, J. S. Caldwell, W. H. Goler, L. W. Oldfield, Tilghman Brown, S. C. Birchmore, W. H. Ferguson, A. F. Goslin, P. J. McIntosh, John E. Allen, J. B. Colbert, J. H. Anderson, Prof. S. G. Atkins, Hon. T. Thomas Fortune and Hon. W. C. Coleman. Revs. E. Geo. Biddle, G. W. Offley, E. H. Curry, J. W. Smith, J. E. Mason, R. H. Stitt, R. S. Rives, P. L. Cuyler, H. Blake, N. A. Crockett, M. H. Ross, J. P. Meacham, John Holliday, H. W. Harris, J. M. Washington, F. M. Jacobs, F. A. Clinton, G. L. Blackwell, Hon. J. C. Dancey, Prof. B. A. Johnson, Hon. H. C. Weden, Hon. J. H. Butler, Mr. E. V. C. Eto and Frederick Douglass.

>Bishop A. WALTERS, *Chairman;*
>Rev. G. W. CLINTON, *Secretary;*
>Rev. E. GEORGE BIDDLE, *Treasurer,*
>Hon. J. C. DANCEY, *Manager.*"

XI

THE CENTENNIAL JUBILEE

"Our fathers, moved by faith and hope,
With spirit meek and low,
Established Zion firm and sure,
One hundred years ago."

THE twentieth Quadrennial session of our General Conference met in State Street Church, Mobile, Ala., May, 1896. It was a notable gathering—three bishops were elected: Drs. G. W. Clinton, Jehu Holliday and J. B. Small. At this session the committee appointed on our One Hundredth Anniversary made its report. The committee stated that Mother Zion had been secured in which to hold the Jubilee and that arrangements had been made to have each church and each Annual Conference contribute to the fund and that excellent prizes had been offered to the church, Presiding Elder and pastor contributing the largest sum of money. It further reported that the following appeals had been sent out:

To all evangelical churches of the United States of America, and to the Methodist bodies of Canada and the British Isles:
Greeting:
In 1796 James Varick and others, because of the

existence of proscription and other conditions which hindered their intellectual development and religious growth, and prevented them from engaging in the work of spreading the cause of Christ and uplifting their fellows according as they felt themselves moved by the spirit of God, withdrew from the Mother Church and formed a separate and distinct organization, out of which has grown the great African Methodist Episcopal Zion Church.

We congratulate ourselves on having had a man of such unselfish motives, sterling qualities and pronounced ability as an organizer and leader, to head this great religious movement; he was the first man of the race to grasp the great idea of a purely Negro religious organization.

During this hundred years our church has grown from a handful to nearly 400,000 communicants, embracing every section of the United States, Canada, a part of Africa and some of the Islands of the Sea. It has taken a foremost part in all movements affecting the moral, intellectual and spiritual welfare of the race.

At the session of the General Conference held at Pittsburgh, Pa., in 1892, it was decided that we should hold our One Hundredth Anniversary in the month of October in 1896 in "Mother Zion" (our first established church in the connection), now situated at the corner of West 10th and Bleecker Streets, New York City, N. Y.

We take this medium through which to inform you of our intention, and to earnestly ask your sympathy and co-operation to make this centennial effort a success in advancing the Redeemer's Kingdom and in the elevation of the race.

It is our purpose to hold a Ten Day Centennial Conference, two sessions each day, at which time papers will be read and subjects discussed as may be agreed upon.

THE CENTENNIAL JUBILEE 91

Every denomination or religious organization is cordially invited to participate with us. We especially invite all Methodist organizations to take part with us.

Each denomination desiring representation will please communicate with Bishop A. Walters, D.D., Chairman, Centennial Committee, No. 353 Bleecker St., New York City, N. Y.

SPECIAL APPEAL

The general appeal to the ministers and members of the A. M. E. Zion Church, and to all others to whom this appeal shall come:

Greeting:

In the Providence of God, we are nearing the close of the first century of our existence as a church organization. The success which has attended our exertions through the century in the spread of churches, in the gathering of converts and in the uplift of the people generally, in their moral and religious life, and in their material prosperity, has been phenomenal.

From a handful of members, not more than sixty, who gathered in New York in 1796, we have increased in membership to 411,768, enlarged our borders until we now control our churches and ministers in thirty-one states, Canada, Africa and the Islands of the Sea.

God has wonderfully blessed our efforts and prospered the work of our hands. Necessary institutions for the better equipment and perpetuity of our work, for which at the beginning of our organization we had neither the means to found, nor the men to fill, have been brought into existence and successfully operated.

We feel reasonable and pardonable pride in the tremendous growth of our church in all of its related branches; and we feel that the membership of the church share in the feeling, and that they may be moved to second all efforts put forth to make the Centennial year not only a success, as far as we are concerned as a church, but as marking a distinct epoch in the history of the race on this continent.

The Jubilee will be held in New York City in October, 1896, continuing ten days. The spiritual and financial success of the celebration will depend upon the united efforts of the ministers, members and friends of Zion Church. Let us pray that the closing year of the century will be marked by a general revival throughout the entire church, and that there will be an ingathering of souls unprecedented in the history of the Connection.

To furnish an opportunity to the members and friends of Zion Church to appropriately express thanks to God and show their loyalty and devotion to His cause, we have deemed it fitting to ask a Centennial THANK OFFERING to enable us to go forward in the work of church extension with renewed confidence at the beginning of the new century.

Knowing the devotion of the churches, and their interest and enthusiasm in this celebration, it is believed that each interested person will gladly embrace this opportunity to consecrate not less than ONE DOLLAR to this cause; and we also look to the generous spirit of a confiding public who have never withheld assistance when fairly and earnestly appealed to for aid.

And upon the celebration and the work of the church generally we invoke the Divine blessing.

Signed for the Centennial Committee by the Committee on Special Appeal: G. W. Offley, W. H. Goler, T. Thomas Fortune, J. S. Caldwell, J. H. Anderson, H. W. Smith, R. S. Rives, Jehu Holliday, F. A. Clinton.

Bishop A. WALTERS, *Chairman;*
Rev. G. W. CLINTON, *Secretary;*
Rev. E. GEO. BIDDLE, *Treasurer;*
Hon. J. C. DANCEY, *Manager.*

THE CENTENNIAL JUBILEE 93

This Centennial was a success in point of attendance, excellency of program and large financial results. It attracted the attention of the American people which no similar race event up to this time had ever attracted in this country. The fame and prominence of those who contributed to its proceedings were world-wide.

The opening sermon was preached by Bishop Charles H. Fowler, LL.D., of the M. E. Church, and the anniversary sermon by Bishop J. W. Hood, D.D., LL.D., the Senior Bishop. Among the prominent men who delivered addresses were Dr. Alex. Crummel, Dr. William Hayes Ward, Rev. Hutchins Bishop, T. Thomas Fortune and a host of others.

Total receipts by Conferences:

New York Conference	$1,318.51
New England Conference	939.77
New Jersey Conference	369.99
Philadelphia and Baltimore Conference	640.63
Genesee (Western N. Y.) Conference	309.39
Central N. C. Conference	595.07
North Carolina Conference	76.18
Alabama Conference	463.37
Georgia Conference	7.75
Michigan and Canada Conference	10.00
West Tennessee and Mississippi Conference	36.00
Missouri Conference	62.00
Florida Conference	87.78
Louisiana Conference	92.05

California Conference 25.25
Arkansas Conference 80.00
Ohio and Alleghany Conference........ 344.45
Kentucky Conference 42.25
Tennessee Conference 61.00
Western N. C. Conference.............. 278.18
Blue Ridge Conference................ 135.45
Virginia Conference 281.00

Centennial Meeting, Asbury Park...... 78.00
Centennial Bazaar 80.55
Received from Carnegie Hall Concert... 533.84
Collection Mother Zion Church......... 150.00
Sale of Souvenirs.................... 200.00
Received from Mr. Dancey............. 254.35

Total ....

Expenditures were equal to the receipts. Of this amount two thousand and twenty-three dollars ($2,023.00) was paid to Bishop T. H. Lomax to be applied on the Varick Memorial Building, Charlotte, N. C. Several churches were aided out of the net proceeds.

Too much praise cannot be given to Bishop J. W. Hood, whose district reported the largest amount of money raised and who helped in many other ways to make the Centennial a success. Honorable J. C. Dancey also deserves to be commended for his valuable assistance.

XII

THE AFRO-AMERICAN COUNCIL

"We hold these truths to be self-evident,—that all men are created equal; that they are endowed by their Creator with certain unalienable rights; that among these are life, liberty and the pursuit of happiness."—*Declaration of Independence.*

"WHAT must we do to be saved"? This was the serious inquiry proposed at the close of the Civil War. The answer came quickly and decisively—Educate—Improve our morals—Get money—and the Party of Lincoln that has added the thirteenth, fourteenth and fifteenth amendments to the Federal Constitution will see that we get our Civil and Political Rights. For it had promised them to us. We forthwith proceeded to educate; to improve our morals; and to get money. And we, indeed, made astonishing progress.

In the midst of this progress, we were suddenly awakened to the fact that the party of Lincoln had sold us out in 1876 in order to secure the presidency. The protection which had been given us in the South and without which it was utterly impossible for us to retain our Civil and

Political rights, had been withdrawn; hence we were left exposed to the wrath of our enemies.

It was apparent to all that something must be done by way of organization, if the race was to be saved. Mr. T. Thomas Fortune, one of the ablest and bravest of our leaders, in a series of articles in the New York *Freeman* (now *Age*), called attention to the deplorable state of affairs and urged the Negroes to organize for their self-protection.

He finally issued the following Appeal:

To the Colored Citizens of the Republic: Being convinced that the time is ripe for the organization of the National Afro-American League, proposed by me two years ago, to successfully combat the denial of our Constitutional and inherent rights, so generally denied or abridged throughout the Republic, and being urged to do so by members of branch leagues all over the country, I, by these presents, issue a call to all the branches of the Afro-American League, and invite all clubs and societies organized to secure the rights of the race, to meet by their representatives in National Convention at Chicago, Ill., Wednesday, January 15, 1890, for the purpose of organizing a National Afro-American League; the basis of Representation to be four delegates for every one hundred members, or one delegate for every twenty-five members, constituting the branch league, club or society, desiring to co-operate in the movement for National organization.

Correspondence from all organizations desiring to join in this movement is requested.

Very respectfully,
T. THOMAS FORTUNE.

New York, November 4, 1889.

THE AFRO-AMERICAN COUNCIL 97

Concurring in this call:
> Alexander Walters, of New York.
> J. Gordon Street, of Massachusetts.
> W. A. Pledger, of Georgia.
> Robert Pelham, Jr., of Michigan.
> Edward E. Cooper, of Indiana.
> H. C. Smith, of Ohio.
> John Mitchell, Jr., of Virginia.
> Magnus L. Robinson, of Virginia.
> J. C. Price, of North Carolina.
> John C. Dancey, of North Carolina.
> Thomas T. Symmons, District of Columbia.
> F. L. Barnett, of Illinois.
> Z. T. Cline, of New Jersey.
> Van N. Williams, of Alabama.
> B. Prillerman, of West Virginia.
> Wm. H. Heard, of Pennsylvania.
> R. K. Sampson, of Tennessee.
> H. M. Morris, of South Carolina.
> James G. McPherson, of Mississippi
>> and others.

The reader will observe that my name appears first on this call, showing my complete sympathy with Mr. Fortune in the organization.

In accordance with the call, the league convened in Chicago, January 15, 1890, and was an enthusiastic gathering. There were twenty-one States represented by a convention of one hundred and forty-one delegates. A national organization was effected, with Rev. J. C. Price, D.D., of Livingstone College, president; T. Thomas Fortune, Esq., editor of New York *Age*, secretary; Lawyer E. H. Morris, Chicago, and George H. Jackson, Esq., treasurer.

For above informations, see *The Afro-American Press*, pages 530, 531, 532.

At the meeting held at Knoxville, Tenn., in 1891, Dr. Price was succeeded in the presidency by Mr. Fortune, but for lack of interest on the part of the masses as well as leaders of the race, there was not another meeting of the league called.

On the 10th of March, 1898, I sent the following appeal to the New York *Age:*

Fellow Citizens: The late outrages perpetrated against Postmasters Loften of Hogansville, Ga., and Baker of Lake City, S. C., for no other reason than their race and color, and having no reason to believe from past experience that the perpetrators will be brought to justice; and further, because there is a determined effort on the part of the white labor unions of the country to exclude the Negro from the industrial avenues in which he can make an honest living, it becomes absolutely necessary that we organize for self-protection.

I therefore move that T. Thomas Fortune, president of the National Afro-American League, call a meeting of the leaders of the race at an early date, to take in consideration the present condition of affairs and suggest a remedy for the same. All who will unite with me in this request please send their names to this paper.

Respectfully,

A. WALTERS,
Bishop of A. M. E. Zion Church.

The following joined in the call:

S. L. Corrothers, Elmira, N. Y.
Edward U. A. Brooks, L.L.M., Elmira, N. Y.
D. W. Jones, Illinois.

THE AFRO-AMERICAN COUNCIL 99

Alexander Davenger, Pennsylvania.
Lewis Black, Pennsylvania.
Frank Wheaton, Minnesota.
John Sims, Iowa.
S. P. Livingstone, Florida.
Roger S. Thompson, Arizona.
William S. Scott, Washington.
William DeCapter, New Mexico.
L. Xavier, New Mexico.
D. W. Wisher, Jersey City, N. J.
C. H. J. Taylor, Atlanta, Ga.
P. Butler Thompkins, A.M., New York City.
A. L. Askew, New York City.
Wm. J. Kelley, Port Jervis, N. Y.
H. T. Johnson, D.D., Philadelphia.
J. W. Smith, D.D., Charlotte, N. C.
J. S. Caldwell, D.D., Philadelphia.
W. H. Davenport, Camden, N. J.
M. L. Blalock, Paterson, N. J.
J. M. Gregory, Principal Industrial School, Bordentown, N. J.
A. J. Warner, D.D., Birmingham, N. J.
J. C. Temple, Jersey City, N. J.
M. R. Franklin, D.D., New York.
F. M. Jacobs, D.D., Brooklyn, N. Y.
J. H. White, D.D., Trenton, N. J.
L. J. Wheeler, Paterson, N. J.
H. L. Jones, Editor of the New York *Pilot*.
James M. Henderson, A.M., D.D., Pres. Morris Brown Col., Atlanta, Ga.
Edward W. Crosby, Buffalo, N. Y.
J. W. Hood, Bishop A. M. E. Zion Church, Fayetteville, N. C.
James H. Matthews, New York City.
Jas. E. Mason, Rochester, N. Y.
John W. Thompson, Rochester, N. Y.
Ida B. Wells Barnett, Pres. Anti-Lynching League, Chicago, Ill.

John Caldwell, Albany, N. Y.
T. T. B. Reed, M.D., Ridgewood, N. J.
Stanley Ruffin, Boston, Mass.
J. R. Robinson, St. Paul, Minn.
A. G. Plummer, Editor of *World,* St. Paul, Minn.
Earnest Lyon, Baltimore, Md.
T. B. Morton, of the Afro-American League of California.
Frederick L. McGhee, attorney at law, St. Paul, Minn.
Judson W. Lyons, Register of the Treasury, Washington, D. C.
William A. Pledger, Georgia.
John W. Cromwell, District of Columbia.
George W. Murray, South Carolina.
R. K. Washington, South Carolina.
James H. Roston, Connecticut.
James A. Wilkins, Connecticut.
Frank Jones, Connecticut.
H. C. Denney, North Carolina.
James E. Hunt, Maryland.
Thomas E. Stevens, Virginia.
William H. Nelson, Virginia.
Charles Turner, Missouri.
Nelson Crews, Missouri.
Henry Bridgewater, Missouri.
William Dye, Missouri.
R. A. Dawson, Illinois.
Robert Davis, 138 Fifth Ave., New York City.
John Mitchell, Jr., Editor of Richmond *Planet.*
J. H. Brice, Richmond, Va.
A. W. Harris, Petersburg, Va.
D. F. Batts, Petersburg, Va.
J. J. Adams, Petersburg, Va.
G. W. Clinton, Bishop A. M. E. Zion Church, Charlotte, N. C.
A. J. Tolbert, Catskill, N. Y.
S. E. Hatton, Binghamton, N. Y.

THE AFRO-AMERICAN COUNCIL 101

J. T. Wilkins, Ravenswood, N. Y.
J. H. Washington, Port Jervis, N. Y.
J. B. S. Capponi, Pres. of American Negro Union, Texarkana, Tex.
J. P. Peaker, Pres. of Sumner League, New Haven, Conn.
James A. Ross, Buffalo, N. Y.
John Quincy Adams, Harrisburg, Pa.
Edwin J. Watkins, Auburn, N. Y.
Prof. W. F. Johnson, Brooklyn, N. Y.
Wm. H. Ferris, Harvard Divinity School, Cambridge, Mass.
Henry A. Spencer, Pres. Douglass League, Rochester, N. Y.
S. P. W. Drew, Long Island City, N. Y.
T. W. Johnson, Brooklyn, N. Y.
Moses Sterrett, Shreveport, La.
F. S. McKeel, Shreveport, La.
Horatio Nelson Rankin, Memphis, Tenn.
Robert B. Robinson, Alexandria, Va.
I. B. Scott, New Orleans, editor *Southwestern Christian Advocate.*
Ethelbert Evans, Troy, N. Y.
Mrs. N. F. Mossell, Philadelphia, Pa.
George H. Wilson, West Asbury Park, N. J.
W. H. Brown, Towanda, Pa.
John C. Dancey, Collector of Customs, Wilmington, N. C.
G. Grant Williams, Hartford, Conn.
John H. True, Goshen, N. Y.
Charles H. Flint. Los Angeles, Cal.
William M. Prime, Buffalo, N. Y.
E. R. Spaulding, Owego, N. Y.
C. C. Crocket, Albuquerque, New Mexico.
George H. Emanuel, Albuquerque, New Mexico.
Wm. B. Bowens, Troy, N. Y.
E. B. Burroughs, Darlington, S. C.
J. P. Sampson, D.D., Philadelphia, Pa.

Magnus L. Robinson, editor of *Leader,* Alexandria, Va.

G. Harold Smith, editor *Public Record,* Atlantic City, N. J.

J. N. Johnson, financial secretary of the Negro National Protective Association of the United States, Washington, D. C.

F. Z. S. Peregrino, editor of Buffalo *Spectator.*

W. N. Walker, New York City.

W. Bishop Johnson, Washington, D. C.

John A. Andrew, Post 234, G. A. R., Commander Samuel E. Sexton, New York City.

J. W. Oscar Garrett, Athens, Tenn.

James T. Gaskill, Tarrytown, N. Y.

I was informed by Mr. Fortune that he would make the call, if I secured one hundred names to my petition, which I did. On August 24, 1898, Mr. Fortune issued the following call:

To Bishop Alexander Walters, Jersey City, N. J.:

My dear Sir:

On the 10th of March last you did me the honor to suggest that I issue, as president, a call for the resurrection and rehabilitation of the Afro-American League, which was organized at Chicago, Ill., January 15, 1890, the second and last annual meeting of which was held at Knoxville, Tenn., in 1892. Since the first publication of your request in the *Age,* March 10th, last, numerous persons, to the number of one hundred fifty, have joined in the request, and their names have been published from time to time, attached to your request, and have therefore become a part of it, attaching national importance to the desire for some organized expression of Afro-American opinion of the conditions which confront the race and which differ but little from those stated by me in 1890, as a suf-

THE AFRO-AMERICAN COUNCIL 103

ficient provocation for calling the Afro-American League at Chicago.

I have given your request long and faithful consideration, and have reached the conclusion that the popular sentiment behind the request does not justify me in acceding to it. There is just as much need of the Afro-American League to-day as there was in 1890; there is even more need for such an organization; but I do not believe that the masses of the race are any more ready and willing to organize local and State Leagues of the National League and to sustain them by moral and financial support than they were in 1890 and 1892. I am therefore not willing to take the responsibility of undertaking the resurrection of the Afro-American League when the chances of effecting a permanent organization are so very doubtful.

But, in deference to the desires of yourself and the persons who have joined you in the request, and after consultation with responsible men and women in all parts of the country, who feel with me that something of an organized nature should be done to stem the tide of wrong and injustice of which the race is made victims, I have decided to call a conference at Rochester, New York, September 15, 1898, to consider existing conditions and to take such action as may be wise, loyal and patriotic for the future, the conference to be composed of those who have joined in the request for the resurrection of the Afro-American League, and who shall determine upon the admission of such others as may appear at Rochester and desire to participate in the work of the conference.

My excuse for calling the conference at Rochester is to take advantage of the race sentiment which will be invoked by the unveiling of a monument to Frederick Douglass, in Rochester, September 14, a city in which Mr. Douglass spent some of the best and happiest and most fruitful years of his life, and one of the freest and most tolerant cities in the Republic, whose hotels and homes and press will receive the conference with open arms and generous hospitality.

Persons desiring to attend the conference should write to Mr. John W. Thompson, P. O. Box 493, Rochester, New York, for railroad rates and hotel accommodations.

Invoking the Divine blessing on the proposed conference, and thanking you, Bishop Walters, and your co-signers for the honor you have done me in your request, I am, with sentiments of high regard,

Yours truly,
T. THOMAS FORTUNE.

New York, August 24, 1898.

The delegates assembled at Rochester on the 15th of September, and the following is a synopsis of the proceedings:

Pursuant to a call of a hundred and fifty prominent representatives of the negro race in the United States, a Conference was held yesterday in the common council chambers to consider the advisability of reviving the old Afro-American League, which was first organized in Chicago early in 1892, but which afterward went out of existence. Two sessions were held yesterday. After thoroughly discussing the need of the organization in order to fight everything that is antagonistic to the race, it was decided not to reorganize the old league, but to form a new one under the name of the National Afro-American Council. Rochester, then, has the distinction of being the birthplace of what may prove a potent factor in the great social problems of this country.

T. Thomas Fortune, having been president of

THE AFRO-AMERICAN COUNCIL 105

the old league, called the Conference to order. Among those present were: Mrs. Helen Douglass, widow of the late Frederick Douglass, and other members of the family; Mrs. Emily Howard, Mrs. Sarah E. Blackall, Mrs. Ida B. Wells Barnett, Chicago; Mrs. L. C. Smith, Washington; Mrs. Jeffreys, president of the Rochester Colored Women's League; Miss Susan B. Anthony; T. Thomas Fortune, editor of the New York *Age;* John H. Smyth, ex-minister to Liberia; Chris J. Perry, editor of the Philadelphia *Tribune;* Bishop Alexander Walters, D.D., of New Jersey; Collector of Customs J. C. Dancey, Wilmington, N. C.; Joseph Dixon, Buffalo; Rev. W. B. Bowens, Troy; John W. Thompson, Rev. A. Alonzo Scott, Rochester. After the Conference had been called to order, Mr. Thompson introduced Mayor Warner, who delivered the address of welcome.

Upon motion of Bishop Walters, Mr. Fortune was made chairman, and Mrs. Barnett, secretary of the meeting. All who wished to become members of the conference were asked to step within the railing, there being no restriction as to color. A brief address was made by Miss Susan B. Anthony, after which the chair appointed the following committees:

Organization: Bishop A. Walters, Charles R. Douglass, John W. Thompson, Mrs. Jeffreys, Rev. W. E. Bowen.

Resolutions: John C. Dancey, Mrs. Sprague, C. J. Perry, Mrs. Ida Wells Barnett, F. S. Cunningham.

The report of the organization committee, as finally adopted, was to the effect that the new organization should be called the National Afro-American Council; that its object should be the amelioration of the colored race, as set forth in the address of the committee to be presented later; that the officers should consist of president, vice-president, secretary and treasurer, with an executive committee of seven; that the national council should consist of five representatives from each State, two of whom should be women; that wherever ten or more persons should be found in sympathy with the objects of the council, they could organize a State council. That the annual fees should be not less than $5.00.

The chair appointed as a committee on nominations, Bishop Walters, W. E. Bowen and Mrs. Jeffreys. They reported in favor of T. Thomas Fortune for president, but Mr. Fortune acknowledged that he had not confidence enough in the race to carry the council on to success, and consequently his name was withdrawn. The officers as finally agreed upon were: President, Bishop Alexander Walters, Jersey City, N. J.; Vice-President, J. C. Dancey, Wilmington, N. C.; Secretary, Mrs. Ida B. W. Barnett, Chicago; Treasurer, John W. Thompson, Rochester.

Executive Committee: John C. Dancey, Mrs. J. W. Barnett, John W. Thompson, Bishop B. W. Arnett, Joseph P. Peaker, Chris Perry, H. T. Kealing.

The committee on address then presented the

THE AFRO-AMERICAN COUNCIL 107

following, which represented the objects of the council, and which was adopted in totum:

LYNCHINGS

The lynching evil is still with us, the most grievous ill to which our race is subjected. Added to the 10,000 victims of mob law, who have been hanged, shot and burned to death without judge or jury within the last twenty years, the year 1897 gave 167 victims. The present year averages about the same number. For the first time in the lynching history this year has furnished a case which will permit action by the United States Government. Reference is made to the case of Postmaster Baker, who was shot and burned to death in Lake City, S. C., because he accepted the office of postmaster in his town. Men have been apprehended and charged with being participators in that dreadful crime, but they are out on bail. We recommend that the executive committee be empowered to carry on the agitation against lynch law throughout the length and breadth of the land and Postmaster Baker's case in particular.

THE CONVICT LEASE SYSTEM

The second greatest infamy from which the race most largely suffers is the convict lease system, in vogue in many of the States of the Union. Men, women and children are slaves to the State, rather than to the individual, with all the horrors of the slave system intensified a hundred fold. We recommend that Mrs. Clarissa O. Keeler of Washington, D. C., be empowered to gather statistics and facts on the subject and present them to this body at its next annual sitting. We especially demand a reformatory for youthful criminals to avoid the prevailing contact of boys and girls with the hardened criminals.

THE SEPARATE CAR LAW

We earnestly recommend that the race, newspapers and ministers of the gospel join hands with us in the crusade against the separate car law, and urge the race to do no traveling, more than is absolutely necessary, in the States where this law obtains. The dollars thrown away in the excursions gotten up too often by our ministers, will go a long way toward fighting this evil.

LABOR COMMISSION

In view of the oppressive discrimination against the Negro in almost all lines of industrial work, it becomes a matter of keenest regret that upon a committee formed to consider industrial questions the colored people should be wholly ignored, and refused all representation. In the North we are barred out of most of the labor organizations, and in the South we are gradually being driven from skilled industries as rapidly as labor unions extend their membership. We are refused the advantages of apprenticeship, denied admission to mercantile establishments: in a word, circumscribed, discriminated against and cruelly oppressed by labor on one hand and capital on the other; the Negro more than any other class of citizens should have its cause heard before the bar of public opinion.

THE PARIS EXPOSITION

We commend to the colored people of the country the efforts now being made to secure for America a worthy exhibit in the Paris Exposition. We would urge hearty co-operation with the plans now being prosecuted to make that Exposition a success, for we recognize that the world will want to see what the

THE AFRO-AMERICAN COUNCIL 109

Negro has done in his thirty years of freedom. In order that the best success in this work may be secured, we ask that our race be not ignored in the formative stages of the Exposition work, but that some representative place be accorded us in which efficient, intelligent and patriotic service can secure for the race the best showing which lies in our power to make. If in the plans of Exposition work already made there exists no opportunity for the special effort here suggested, we recommend that a committee be appointed by this conference to present the matter to Congress, for the purpose of securing a stated appropriation in order that the progress of the race may be shown in the Paris Exposition.

CUBAN IMMIGRATION

We recognize the possibilities which open up to American enterprise and energy in Cuba and the newly-acquired territory of our nation. We believe that special facilities exist there for rapid development and substantial success of plans and purposes prosecuted by colored Americans, and we commend an intelligent survey of the field and prompt action in taking front place with other Americans who shall seek fortune in that new territory.

The executive committee was empowered to draw up the Constitution and by-laws and agreed upon a place for the next meeting. Adjournment was taken after the adoption of resolutions thanking the common council for the use of the rooms and the people and press of Rochester for the cordial welcome extended to the members of the conference.

THE WASHINGTON, D. C., MEETING

Owing to the fact that the meeting at Rochester was not largely attended, and the organization not fully completed, it was thought advisable to call another meeting in the near future to finish the work. Therefore the following call was issued, November 1, 1898:

To the members that were enrolled at the formation of the Council at Rochester, N. Y., September 15, 1898, and all the signers of the call for said meeting, and all who are in sympathy with the object of the Council which is the amelioration of the condition of the Afro-American race, and are willing to contribute $5.00 annually towards carrying out of the purposes of the Council:

You are hereby requested to meet at Washington, D. C., on Thursday, December 29, 1898. If any apology is needed for the issuing of this call of the Afro-American Council so soon after its formation, I hope the following reasons will be satisfactory:

First: A large number of the leaders of the race who were anxious to attend the convention held at Rochester were prevented from doing so because of the limited time between the issuing of the call (August 24) and the date of the convention (September 15).

Second: The place of meeting (Rochester, N. Y.) was considered by many as too far removed from the masses of our people, where the majority of our leaders reside, necessarily entailing considerable expense. Mr. Fortune, who issued the call for the Rochester meeting, recognizing this fact, gave the following as his reason for doing so:

"My excuse for calling the meeting at Rochester is to take advantage of the race sentiment which will be invoked by the unveiling of the monument of Fred-

THE AFRO-AMERICAN COUNCIL 111

erick Douglass in Rochester, September 14, a city in which Mr. Douglass spent some of the best and happiest and most fruitful years of his life and one of the freest and most tolerant cities in the Republic, whose hotels, homes and press will receive the conference with open arms and generous hospitality."

Third: We will not have sufficient time to finish up the business of the Council as satisfactorily as desired. These reasons make it necessary that another meeting be called in a more central locality to consummate the work so auspiciously begun at Rochester, giving ample time between the issuing of the call and the date of the meeting for all needed preparation.

The continuation of brutal lynchings, unjust discriminations on railroads and in hotels, restaurants and labor unions, the attempted disfranchisement of Afro-Americans in several of the Southern States and a host of other obstacles which are thrown in the way of our moral, financial and educational progress, make it absolutely necessary that we organize and perpetuate an organization for self-protection.

The Afro-American press is almost a unit in its demand for a national organization which has for its objects a fair representation in the government of the country, local, state and national; to resist by all legal and reasonable means mob and lynch law, of which we are made the principal victims, and to insist upon the arrest and punishment of all such offenders against our legal rights; to resist the tyrannical usages of railroads, steamboats and other corporations, and the violent and insulting conduct of their employees; to labor for the reformation of our penal institutions, where barbarous, cruel and unchristian treatment of convicts is practiced; to secure a more equitable distribution of school funds; to insist on a health emigration from terror-ridden districts to other and more law-abiding sections; to encourage all kinds of business enterprises, etc.

My reason for calling the National Council during holiday week is that the delegates may take advantage of the reduced rates made during that time.

All communications must be addressed to Edward E. Cooper, president of the District of Columbia Branch of the National Afro-American Council, 459 C Street, North West, Washington, D. C..

(Signed)   A. WALTERS,
President.

Jersey City, N. J., Nov. 1, 1898.

In pursuance of the above call, on December 29, at 11 A.M., the Afro-American Council assembled at Metropolitan Baptist Church, R Street, between 12th and 13th Streets, Washington, D. C., with Bishop Walters, who presided. A very large congregation was present. After the devotional exercises the presiding officer stated the object of the meeting. Several committees were appointed; chief among them was the committee on "Address to the Country," which consisted of T. Thomas Fortune, Bishop A. Grant, Hon. H. P. Cheetam, recorder of deeds, District of Columbia; Judson W. Lyons, Register of Treasury; J. W. Shay, Alabama; Mrs. Ida B. Wells Barnett, Illinois; W. A. Pledger, Georgia; John Mitchell, Jr., Virginia; J. P. Peaker, Connecticut; Bishop G. W. Clinton, North Carolina; R. H. Terrell, District of Columbia.

The following objects were adopted as principles of the Council:

THE AFRO-AMERICAN COUNCIL 113

OBJECTS

ARTICLE II.

The object of this organization shall be:

(1) To investigate and make an impartial report of all Lynchings and other outrages perpetrated upon American Citizens.

(2) To assist in testing the constitutionality of laws which are made for the express purpose of oppressing the Afro-Americans.

(3) To promote the work of securing legislation which in the individual States shall secure to all citizens the rights guaranteed them by the 13th, 14th, and 15th Amendments of the Constitution of the United States.

(4) To aid in the work of Prison Reform.

(5) To recommend a healthy migration from terror-ridden sections of our land to States where law is respected and maintained.

(6) To encourage both industrial and higher education.

(7) To promote business enterprises among the people.

(8) To educate sentiment on all lines that specially affect our race.

(9) To inaugurate and promote plans for the moral elevation of the Afro-American people.

(10) To urge the appropriation for School Funds by the Federal Government to provide education for citizens who are denied school privileges by discriminating State laws.

One of the main features of the Convention was the following address by the Presiding Officer:

THE TRIALS AND ACHIEVEMENTS OF THE AFRO-AMERICAN RACE

It is our misfortune to live among a people whose laws, traditions and prejudices have been against us for centuries. Indeed, it has ever been the policy of a certain class of Americans to keep the Negro down.

As far back as Revolutionary times, when the nation was struggling for its independence from Great Britain, when help was needed and should have been gladly accepted from any source, especially from the free blacks of the country, their enlistment as soldiers was bitterly opposed by the army officers as well as civilians. In October, 1775, General Thomas wrote the following letter to Mr. John Adams:

"I am sorry to hear that any prejudices should take place in any Southern colony in respect to the troops raised in this. I am certain that the insinuations you mention are injurious, if we consider with what precipitation we are obliged to collect an army. We have some Negroes; but I look on them, in general, as equally serviceable with other men for fatigue; and in action many of them have proved themselves brave."

As to the slaves, they were not allowed to enlist in the army at that time. Before the first great battle of the Revolution had been fought, the following resolution was adopted by the Committee of Safety:

"Resolved, That it is the opinion of this committee, that as the contest now between Great Britain and the Colonies are determined to maintain, that the admission of any persons, as soldiers, into the army now raising, but such as are Freemen, will be inconsistent with the principles that are supported, and reflect dishonor on this Colony; and that no Slaves be admitted into this army upon any consideration whatever."

This policy was followed until General Washington and other officers discovered that they were unnecessarily prolonging the war, thus increasing loss of life and treasures.

The British promised freedom to all slaves who would enlist in their ranks and 30,000 enrolled under their banner; it was only their great desire for freedom that caused them to do so. The Americans enlisted in all only about five thousand; they excluded from their ranks thousands of able-bodied men who were willing and anxious to help them. Those who were allowed to enlist did yeoman service for the cause of independence, and won distinction at Boston Common, Bunker Hill and Yorktown. It is to the everlasting shame of the Revolutionary Fathers that after these men had fought so nobly to achieve the independence of their country, many of them were re-enslaved and oppressed by the very people who themselves had struggled so bravely to free themselves from oppression.

Thus you see the Negro was not treated fairly, but every possible effort was put forth to keep him down.

Strenuous efforts were also made to keep the Negro out of the war of 1812, and were successful until General Jackson saw the necessity of enlisting them in 1814. The following Proclamation explains itself:

Headquarters, Seventh Military District,

Mobile, September 21, 1814.

To the Free Colored Inhabitants of Louisiana:

Through a mistaken policy you have heretofore been deprived of a participation in the glorious struggle for national rights in which our country is engaged. This no longer shall exist. As sons of freedom you are now called upon to defend our most inestimable blessing. As Americans your country looks with confidence to her adopted children for a valorous support, as a faithful return for the advantages enjoyed under her mild and equitable government. As fathers, husbands and brothers, you are summoned to rally around the standard of the Eagle, to defend all which is dear in existence. To assure you of the sincerity of my intentions and my anxiety to engage your invaluable services to our country, I have communicated my wishes to the Governor of Louisiana, who is fully informed as to the manner of enrollment, and will give you every necessary information on the subject of this address.

ANDREW JACKSON,
Major-General Commanding."

(Niles Register, vol. vii, p. 205.)

Again, every plan that ingenuity could devise was inaugurated to keep the Negro from becoming a soldier in the late Civil War, but God had decreed that he should be given an opportunity to fight for his freedom; therefore Mr. Lincoln and all the officers of the Union Army, sustained by the most bitter protests of the South, could not keep him out of the War.

On the 8th of July, 1862, the Committee of Military Affairs, through its chairman, Senator Henry Wilson, of Massachusetts, reported from that committee a bill authorizing the arming of Negroes as a part of the army; the bill finally passed both houses and received the approval of the President on the 17th of July, 1862. In discussing this bill, Mr. Sherman (Rep.) of Ohio, said:

"The question arises whether the people of the United States, struggling for national existence, should not employ these blacks for the maintenance of the Government. The policy heretofore pursued by the officers of the United States has been to repel this class of people from our lines, to refuse their services. They would have made the best spies, and yet they have been driven from our lines."

Mr. Fessenden (Rep.) of Maine, said:

"I tell the President from my place here as a senator, I tell the generals of our army, they must reverse their practices and their course of proceeding on this subject. I advise it here from my place—treat your enemies as enemies, as the worst enemies, and avail yourselves like men of every power which God has placed in your hands to accomplish your purpose within the rules of civilized warfare."

THE AFRO-AMERICAN COUNCIL 117

Mr. Rice (War Dem.) of Minnesota declared that:
"Not many days can pass before the people of the United States. The North must decide upon one of two questions; we have either to acknowledge the Southern Confederacy as a free and independent nation and that speedily; or we have as speedily to resolve to use all the means given us by the Almighty to prosecute this war to a successful termination. The necessity for action has arisen. To hesitate is worse than criminal."

Mr. Wilson said:

"The senator from Delaware, as he is accustomed to do, speaks boldly and decidedly against the proposition. He asks if American soldiers will fight if we organize colored men for military purposes. Did not American soldiers fight at Bunker Hill with Negroes in the ranks, one of whom shot down Major Pitcairn as he mounted the works? Did not American soldiers fight at Red Bank with a black regiment from New Jersey? Did not they fight on the battlefield of Rhode Island with that black regiment, one of the best and bravest that ever trod the soil of this continent. Did not American soldiers fight at Fort Griswold with black men? Did they not fight with black men in almost every battlefield of the Revolution? Did not the men of Kentucky and Tennessee, standing on the lines of New Orleans, under the eyes of Andrew Jackson, fight with colored battalions whom he had summoned to the field, and whom he thanked publicly for their gallantry in hurling back a British foe? It is all talk, idle talk, to say that the volunteers who are fighting the battles of this country are governed by any such narrow prejudices or bigotry. These prejudices are the result of the teachings of demagogues and politicians, who have for years undertaken to delude and deceive the American people, and to demean and degrade them." (See Black Phalanx.)

As a result of this able discussion the bill was passed

and the Negroes were enlisted as soldiers. We are all acquainted with their deeds of valor. The silent monuments at Miliken's Bend, Fort Wagner, Port Hudson and Petersburg speak more eloquently than I can of the bravery and faithfulness of our men. It is evident to any one who will give consideration to this question that it was the Lord who opened the way for the Negro to fight for his freedom.

Our next great achievement was that of our emancipation. The opposition to our emancipation was still greater than the opposition to our enlistment as soldiers. All kinds of compromises were enacted in order to placate the South and enable them to retain their slaves. The greatest intellects of that time were enlisted on the side of the perpetuation of slavery. Good men at the North said during the days of the anti-slavery agitation that it was best for the Negroes and all concerned that the institution of slavery be let alone. They declared that the development of the slaveholder's conscience would finally reach a point where he would of his own accord liberate the slaves.

William Lloyd Garrison, Phillips, Douglass, John Brown and a host of others saw it in a different light, and continued amid howling mobs to agitate the immediate abolition of the slaves. Mr. Lincoln, himself the great emancipator, said, if he could save the Union without freeing the slaves, he would do so. But God had ordered differently, and to the surprise and astonishment of friends and foes and to the great joy of the Negro, this very President, who had been so reluctant to make the Negro a soldier, as a war measure, emancipated him; and to confirm him in his citizenship the 13th Amendment was passed, December 18, 1865, which reads as follows:

Section 1. Neither slavery nor involuntary servitude, except as a punishment for crime whereof the party shall have been duly convicted, shall exist within the

THE AFRO-AMERICAN COUNCIL 119

United States, or any place subject to their jurisdiction.

Section 2. Congress shall have power to enforce this article by appropriate legislation. It does not take a philosopher to discover the hand of God in it.

Our next victory was our enfranchisement. When this was mooted it created a storm of opposition. The white men of the South and their sympathizers held up their hands in holy horror; they said it meant the placing of the Negro's heel on the white man's neck. The Southern press and a great many influential papers of the North were loud in their protests against the enfranchisement of the Negro; but to the far-seeing, the prognosticators of the signs of the times, it was discovered that "The Eternal Powers" had decided that the Negro should be further elevated: hence his enfranchisement, which was accomplished by the passing of the Fifteenth Amendment, adopted March 30, 1868, and which reads as follows:

Section 1. The right of the citizens of the United States to vote shall not be denied or abridged by the United States or by any State on account of race, color or previous condition of servitude.

Section 2. The Congress shall have power to enforce the provisions of this article by appropriate legislation.

In this achievement the favor of God towards us is plainly seen. Everything imaginable has been done in the Southland to defeat the purpose of this enactment. When mild intimidation failed, they have terrorized Negro neighborhoods by parading with shotguns, Winchesters and lately with Gatling guns. When these measures failed they have resorted to wholesale murder. The absurd cry of "White supremacy" and "Negro domination," of which we hear so much, has been raised for political purposes only. General Wade Hampton, of South Carolina, said in a speech a few years ago:

"I have no fear of Negro domination—a cry used

only to arouse race prejudice and to put the coming convention under control of the ring which now dominates our State. The Negroes have acted of late with rare moderation and liberality, and if we meet them in the same spirit they have shown, they will aid in selecting good representatives for the convention. I for one am willing to trust them, and they ask only the rights guaranteed to them by the Constitution of the United States and that of our own State, and that ought to be allowed them."

Ex-Senator Joseph E. Brown, of Georgia, speaking on the same subject, says:

"They (the Negroes) have exercised the rights of freemen with a moderation that probably no other race would have done."

The white people of the South will have a hard task to make the world believe that it is to protect the honor of their women and to prevent "Negro domination" that they are obliged to resort to mob violence; and if they think that the white people of the North sympathize with them in their dastardly outrages on innocent colored people, they are greatly mistaken. The New York *Press* of November 11, 1898, says:

"Office hunger seeks to cloak itself under a solicitude for the rights of property and the good repute of women, burning and butchering for its altars and its fires, when it is really after nothing but political pap."

Dr. William Hayes Ward, Editor of the New York *Independent*, one of the most influential weeklies in America, has written several excellent and fair editorials on the real causes of the recent race riots in North and South Carolina. In the issue of November 24, 1898, he says:

"For some weeks before election the politicians began to lash the popular prejudice against 'Negro rule' until it reached a frenzy past belief, and against all reason. The old oligarchy felt their power slipping away; the ignorant whites could not endure to see a

THE AFRO-AMERICAN COUNCIL 121

Negro's vote counted. The sectional prejudice had been wearing thin since the Spanish war, and something must be done to revive it in another form."

Speaking further of the race riots in Wilmington, he said:

"The total officers of the county were, exclusive of the justices of the peace, twenty-nine, twenty of whom were white and nine colored, the Register of Deeds and Coroner being the only important offices held by the Negroes. It will be seen how hypocritical is the cry of Negro domination."

Quite a number of the most influential dailies and weeklies of the North have seen through these subterfuges (all official positions in the South for democrats, destruction of the republican party in the South, of which we form the major part, and antipathy towards the Negro), and are bold in denouncing them.

Hon Judson Lyon, Register of the United States Treasury, in his able article in the New York *Herald* of December 4, 1898, has shown by actual count of the offices held by colored men in North Carolina that Negro domination was impossible—indeed, absurd. He says, speaking on this subject:

"We hear it all around that 'the blacks are in control of the State—in complete control'; it was 'Negro domination,' overbearing in its insolence; it could not be endured, and, hence, on the cry of 'white supremacy' white and black men alike were driven from the State.

"In the Legislature of North Carolina there are 120 Representatives and fifty Senators, making a total of 170. I have the exact figures; there are seven members of the House and two Senators, nine colored Representatives all told, in those bodies, not one-eighteenth of the members. Not one in a State office—I mean in the Governor's cabinet or an office of that kind. Under this showing there could be no Negro domination at Raleigh, the capital. One man could not dominate eighteen unless by their acquiescence.

"In the city of Wilmington, where so much innocent blood has been spilled and so many valuable lives taken by that furious mob, see what are the facts:

"It is said that the city never had a cleaner, more honest and upright set of officials.

"As the crowd which calls itself the democracy, and which made speeches with Winchesters and scattered campaign literature with rapid-firing guns, has never successfully denied this, it must be true."

Says he further:

"The Charleston *News and Courier,* perhaps, strikes the nail on the head in its terrible denunciation of the mob, when it declares that it was simply the work of the baser elements of the community—killing and destroying without cause, without provocation and without any shadow of excuse."

We are aware that there is a vicious element of poor, thriftless and ignorant whites, who will not make any advancement themselves and are envious of the advancement made by the Negro, and who are determined to retard his further progress if they can. The following from the Greenville (S. C.) *News* is painful to the Negroes of this nation, who have done so much to make it what it is, and whose valor in saving the Rough Riders at San Juan and El Caney is being heralded to the world:

"As for the Negro, we give him the same advice we have given him for years. He has no rights in this country when the race feeling is aroused—not even the ordinary rights of humanity. Those of us who want to see him have at least the protection that is given to animals can do nothing for him and he can do nothing for himself, for when the color line is made and the race feeling is aroused he will find all of us arrayed against him. For his sake and ours, to save his life and our honor and sense of decency and manhood, let him go somewhere, anywhere away from us."

All other peoples are welcome here except the ever loyal Negro; he is wanted gone because he is black. Shame!

Because of the antagonism of the Southern Whites towards the Negro it has been suggested by some of our leaders as well as some of the whites, that the Negroes in that section withdraw from politics altogether. In my opinion this would be a very unwise step. The Negro is a citizen and interested in the welfare of his country; therefore it is his duty to vote.

The Negroes in the South are accumulating property rapidly and are therefore liable to taxation; the only weapon which they possess to protect themselves against unjust taxation, etc., is the franchise.

Again, it would be a confirmation of the statement made by our enemies when we were given the right of suffrage that we lacked manhood and hence were unworthy of enfranchisement. To surrender our franchise would be base ingratitude to the white heroes now dead who labored so earnestly and suffered so much to have it granted us. We would lose the respect of those living who aided us in obtaining this powerful weapon of defence. And lastly, it would be rank cowardice in us to do such a thing.

We do not object to the franchise being limited by educational and property qualifications, so long as the poor and illiterate whites and blacks are equally affected thereby, but we do object to being disfranchised solely on account of color and race antipathy.

It is unreasonable and unchristian to debar the Negro from holding office on account of his color; therefore it would be unwise to yield to the prejudice of our enemies by giving up all offices to white men. Then in the majority of cases Afro-Americans who hold offices in the South are mulattoes, some of them so white that you can hardly distinguish them from the whites, so all this hue and cry about "big, black, burly Negro officials dominating over the whites" is bosh.

Senator McLaurin, of South Carolina, and a number of others assert that the Negro should not hold office because he is not a large taxpayer. They forget that a large majority of officials who hold minor offices in our larger cities, both North and South, pay but a small fraction of the taxes; this is especially true of the Tammany Hall officials of New York City. A little consideration of the matter will convince any one that our taxes are commensurate with the offices which we hold; hence the argument of excluding us from office because we are non-taxpayers falls to the ground. Race antagonism, and not taxes, is the thing that keeps us out of office.

There are a great many white people in this country who believe that anything above a menial position is too good for a Negro; as to wages, it is thought by them that any amount above $1.00 per day is too much for him.

The greatest care should be exercised on our part in the selection of men to fill public positions; we cannot afford to nominate inefficient men for office; deficiencies which are tolerated in white men will not be tolerated in black ones, and in order to succeed we must put forward only the capable. Our future success as office-holders depends upon our courage and discretion along this line.

After all, the real question which confronts us is, shall the Negro be granted equal rights in the United States of America? I believe that he will, but it will take him a long while to gain it. It took 240 years for his complete personal emancipation and a hundred years to secure his standing as a soldier; it is nonsense to think he can obtain his complete political, civil and social rights within thirty-five years, or even fifty years; if he receives them in a hundred years he will do well.

THE AFRO-AMERICAN COUNCIL

Let us improve our morals, educate ourselves, work, agitate and wait on the Lord.

Since the Lord has brought us face to face with this great question of equality, and since "premonitory mutterings," indeed, all the indications from the Divine side convince us that He is leading on in this as in the other great events through which He has so miraculously and triumphantly brought us after a long and severe struggle, it is our duty to follow where He leads.

There has always been confusion, strife and often bloodshed just before the successful consummation of great movements, but the leaders did not back down; indeed they could hardly have done so had they desired. When Moses went to Pharaoh and said to him, thus saith the Lord, let my people go, instead of harkening to the command he increased their burdens, thinking it was the proper thing to do to defeat the purpose of the Almighty. The Hebrews murmured and were ready to stone their leaders because their burdens were increased. They desired to be let alone, as did their oppressors; just as many of the colored and white people in the South are wishing to-day. But such a thing was impossible, the time for deliverance had come, the issue was on, and God carried it to a successful finish.

Christianity met with the same opposition. The stake, the rack and every other means of torture that wicked ingenuity could devise were inaugurated to stop its onward march, but it availed nothing, as the great Jehovah was leading it on.

The entire Roman Catholic Church endeavored to retard the Protestant movement inaugurated by Luther, but was unable to do so because it was under Divine control.

All sorts of obstacles were employed to hinder the progress of the anti-slavery movement, but did the leaders abandon the field? No.

Mr. Douglass relating his experience said:

"I was doomed by an inveterate prejudice against color to insult and outrage on every hand; denied the privileges and courtesies common to others in the use of the most humble means of conveyance; shut out from the cabins of steamboats; refused admission into respectable hotels; caricatured, scorned, scoffed at, mocked, maltreated with impunity by any one, no matter how black his heart, so he had a white skin."

William Lloyd Garrison and Wendell Phillips were mobbed in liberty-loving Boston. In Cincinnati, Birney's printing press and type were thrown into the Ohio River and the Negroes for days were hunted like beasts. In Alton, Lovejoy was shot while defending his printing press, and the cultured Sumner was assaulted under the very dome of the Capitol. Did they surrender, throw up their hands and say like some are saying now, "we can do nothing to help ourselves"? No! They dared not stop, for they were but the instruments in the hand of God and it was His cause that He was carrying on to success through them. Should we through cowardice prove false to the trust committed to our hands, we should become recipients of the maledictions of the heroes who so faithfully championed our cause, instead of their blessings.

I cannot understand some of our so-called friends who advise us to be quiet and let the white man have his way. Shall we remain silent when the President of the United States, who could not have been elected without our votes, is utterly silent in his last message to Congress concerning the outrages in North and South Carolina and other parts of the country? Remain silent when the Governor of Illinois threatens to blow Negroes to pieces with Gatling guns if they dare to take the places of white strikers who have refused to work? Silent while the officials of the States of North and South Carolina admit they are powerless to protect us in our rights? Silent while Mississippi, Louisiana and South Carolina by statutory

THE AFRO-AMERICAN COUNCIL 127

enactments have practically disfranchised their Negro population, and other States are preparing to do the same? Shall we not speak out when innocent men and women of our race are burned at the stake, hung to the limbs of trees and shot down like dogs? Shall we look on indifferently while our women are insulted and outraged by Negro-hating white men? Shall we say nothing while thousands in the rural districts in the South are robbed of their meagre earnings?

Were we to remain silent under such circumstances we would be unworthy of the name freemen. While I advise action, I at the same time advise prudent action. There can be no real peace in America until this problem is solved, and solved according to the rules of equity. The South must be willing to do unto the Negro as they would have the Negro do unto them.

This nation with all its faults is pre-eminently a Christian nation. The leaven of Christianity (humanity) is at work, and will not cease its work until this whole country is permeated with the humanitarian spirit.

The late Bishop Haygood, of Georgia, says:

"The preponderance of Christian principle and sentiment has done more to save us than any other characteristic of our people or government."

Since the American conscience has been equal to the emergencies of the past we have every reason to believe that it will be equal to any crisis that may come in the future. We, your brethren in black, appeal to this powerful, enlightened Christian conscience, to this humanitarian spirit which has caused this nation to do so much for Cuba, Hawaii and the Philippine Islands, to help us to remove the hindrances which are in the way of our fullest development.

There is no need of our despairing on account of this problem. We have agencies in our possession that will go a long way in the solution of it, the most important of which is the school-house. This potent factor has done as much, if not more, than any other agency at our command to raise us to our present status of power and influence. Education is the sun whose powerful rays of character, industry, self-reliance and patience will ultimately thaw the tremendous iceberg of American prejudice which has chilled us for more than two centuries. Let no one think for a moment that we can have too much sun; the more heat the sooner will the iceberg disappear. We should gladly welcome all educational agencies, whether classical, scientific, industrial or otherwise, that will aid us in the solution of this problem.

I am aware that we have made great progress along educational lines, as is evidenced by the high honors taken by Afro-Americans from the wealthiest and most influential institutions of this country, by the numerous schools and colleges which are being efficiently managed and taught by our colored educators, by the creditable civil service examinations which are being passed daily by members of our race, and by thoughtful and scholarly newspaper and magazine articles written by our race, which are being published continuously in the best periodicals of the land. Still, we must not be unmindful of the fact that the great mass of Negroes are in ignorance, and in order to solve this problem this mass must be reached and made intelligent.

Since the large majority of ignorance is in the South, and the South is too poor or too selfish to appropriate sufficient money to enlighten its great mass of Negro voters, it is therefore the duty of the Federal Government to appropriate money to give to this class of people a common school education, supplemented by an industrial education. We make this plea on the ground that adequate provisions for our enlightenment as voters are denied us on account of our color and previous condition.

Another important factor in our development is industry. Well do I remember that immediately after the emancipation when the leaders of the race would visit our churches and schools, they would invariably tell the boys and girls in their lectures that they were not to do as their fathers and mothers had done; that they should not be content with menial positions but aim high. The young people understood by that they were not to do manual labor as their parents had done, but to enter the professions; as a result the professions are overcrowded and we have a number of idlers. "We began at the top instead of the bottom." Our foundation being defective the superstructure could not be otherwise than defective. We must begin at the bottom— become scientific farmers.

The moment this is suggested some one is ready to say, "We have always been on the farm." That is true, but generally as the "bossed" and not the "bosses" of the farm. The true farmer is the man who does the thinking; as yet we have not entered largely into that kind of business.

The Negro farmer will create a position for the Negro merchant, and the Negro farmer and merchant will create a position for the Negro manufacturer, etc. Support for the Negro minister, doctor, lawyer and all professional men will necessarily follow.

In the beginning instead of dignifying labor we degraded it by teaching the educated boys and girls to scorn manual labor. In my community (Louisville, Ky.) girls without a dollar were ashamed to have young men see them at washing and ironing, and the young men were ashamed to have the girls see them at manual labor. Thus you see false pride was encouraged. Instead of taking knowledge of the Pilgrim Fathers and starting from the bottom, where they did, we took knowledge of the merchants, manufacturers and capitalists who surrounded us and tried to follow them without having laid a like foundation.

It is unfair in our white critics, however, to condemn our educated class of thriftless who aspire to be professionals, mechanics, etc., because they do not all become farmers. Before they censure them let them remove the ban of prejudice, open the doors of factories, mills and machine shops and give them a fair chance. Then if they still remain idle their condemnation will be just.

Let us make the very best of our opportunities along all lines of industry. Notwithstanding all the disadvantages under which we have labored, having been robbed of thousands of dollars by the many unjust systems in operation in the Southland, we have accumulated over $400,000,000 worth of property, real and personal. The thing for us to do is to continue to buy land and to build and improve homes, thus becoming more and more independent.

The next agency in the uplift of the Negro is character. *Talks for the Times* says:

"To estimate fairly their (the Negroes') improvement in this direction it would be necessary to realize, if possible, the depth of degradation to which two hundred and fifty years of thraldom had sunk them, and to take into consideration at the same time the fact that the moral nature of man everywhere and among all people is by far the most difficult to train. This being so, what must be the task to repair it, after it has been bruised and maimed and twisted and gnarled and distorted? A crooked limb by proper application may be straightened. A bone of the body may be broken and set and become even stronger in the fractured parts; but men cannot sin and be strong. The violation of the moral law means in every instance the sapping of moral foundations, the weakening of the moral nature. When, therefore, I consider by what process during two centuries the moral groundwork of my people was undermined and shaken, it is no wonder that to-day many of them are found immoral. The greater wonder is that their moral perception has not been entirely swept away. Many people, however, and those

THE AFRO-AMERICAN COUNCIL 131

especially who stigmatize us as a race peculiarly immoral, do not reason in this way. They do not seem to realize that slavery was a school ill adapted to the producing of pure and upright characters. Can you rob a man continually of his honest earnings and not teach him to steal? Can you ignore the sanctity of marriage and the family relations and not inculcate lewdness? Can you constantly govern a man with the lash and expect him always to speak the truth? If you can do these things then, verily, are my people dishonest, impure and untruthful. But our enemies demand of us perfection. They are unreasonable. They require among us in twenty short years a state of moral rectitude which they themselves, with far more favorable opportunities, have not realized in one hundred times twenty. They are unphilosophical, for they do not perceive that diseases are more quickly contracted than cured."

It is our imperative duty, notwithstanding the bad examples which have been set by some of the whites in this country, to eliminate as far as possible all the immoralities of our race. We should create a healthy public sentiment among us on this line; this can be done by refusing to support immoral ministers, teachers, politicians and all other leaders. Let us raise the standard of morality among us. The following is from the late Dr. Alexander Crummell of our own city:

"Now, if the Negro race in this nation wish to become a people; if they are anxious to prove themselves a stable, saving and productive element in this great Republic; if they are ambitious of advancement in all lines of prosperity, of intelligence, of manly growth and spiritual development, they must fall back upon this grand power of human being—character. They must make this the main and master aim of all high endeavor. They must strive to free themselves from false notions, pernicious principles and evil habits. They must exert themselves to the adoption of correct and saving ideas. They must lift themselves up to superior modes of living. They must introduce as permanent and abiding factors of their life the qualities of thrift, order, discipline, virtue and purity."

Character when combined with intelligence is omnipotent, and has slain more giants of prejudice than any other agency under heaven.

Finally, at the time of our emancipation it was said that we were not capable of providing for ourselves and would soon die out. The wish was father to the thought. But instead of dying out, while in 1860 there were 4,449,201 Negroes, to-day we number 10,000,000, having more than doubled our population in forty years. It is apparent to all that we are not dying out.

Again it was said at the time of our emancipation that we would never accumulate property; we have been a sore disappointment to our enemies along this line, as it has already been stated that we have accumulated over $400,000,000 worth of property.

Again, it was said that the Negro mind was not susceptible of intellectual development, and this in the face of the fact that he was debarred from intellectual opportunities for centuries; indeed, in some parts of the country it was a crime, punishable by law, to even teach the Negro to read. His intellectual achievements during the last thirty-five years have given the lie to that statement.

Dr. Gregg, in his discourse at Lafayette Avenue Presbyterian Church on Sunday, December 18th, said:

"I hear it said that the weakness is inherent in the black race; that Anglo-Saxons could not have been kept in subjection for two centuries and a half. Yet history shows that for five successive centuries the Anglo-Saxons were in slavery in Europe and their freedom finally came from outside. Only one race won its freedom unaided, by its own sword, and that was the black race of San Domingo. We have abolished personal slavery. Let us in no form nullify our act by fraud; let us not rob our black citizen of his rights."

Bishop Haywood, speaking of the treatment of the white men to the Negro, says:

"I must teach the Negro to respect my rights; I do this best by respecting his. I must teach him to respect and keep his contracts; to do this I must respect and keep mine. I must teach him to obey law and to respect authority; to do this I must set the example. I must teach him to 'rule well his own house'; to do this I must show him, not simply teach him, how. I must teach him to speak the truth; to do this I must speak the truth to him; I must teach him honesty; to do this I must be honest. I must teach him purity in his own life and in all his family relations; to do this I must let him see that I respect and keep the law of chastity. I must teach him the sin and ruin of drunkenness; to do this I must keep the demon from my own lips and from my house. I must teach him the sanctity of a freedman's ballot; to do this I must myself vote as an honest man upon my conscience, only for good men, only for good measures, neither buying or selling votes, not cheating in any way, by terror, by violence, by 'ballot stuffing,' by false counting, by false returns or by any method known to demagogues of any land or race."

With this I submit the case.

This address was enthusiastically received. After much discussion, the following address to the country was adopted and issued:

Your committee, to whom was referred the question of considering the present status of the Afro-American race and of making recommendations therefor, for the consideration of the Afro-American people and the people of the United States in general, beg leave to report as follows:

In the present condition of the race, which is abnormally disturbed in one section of the country and comparatively composed in the other three, it is easy to reach the conclusion that we cannot arrive at the desired ends wholly through any one method. There are certain things which those of us who live in the South can accomplish and certain other things which those of us who live in the North can accomplish. We may take different methods to reach the same ends, but the results will be for the common advantage.

In the North the work of agitation, of protest and petition and of political conduct is essential to the cause. The Northern and Western mind needs to be constantly agitated upon our grievances and accurately informed as to their nature and extent. In the South the work of education and internal development can best be determined and carried on by the wise men of us in the Southern States who have done so much since the War of the Rebellion to pave the way for our future status as men and citizens in all the walks of life. We think that it is important that this view of the matter should not be lost sight of for a moment.

We must be broad and liberal in our policy and interpretation of the intentions of all members of the race who have capacity and probity, and who are working for the general good.

The vast extent of our country and the multiplicity of interests and the local prejudices of any sort, outgrowing from phenomenal ethnic differentiations, which must have proper time for inevitable assimilation, makes imperative a broad toleration among us of the difference of opinion as to the best ways and means to secure the best results in given localities, which must determine the final result for weal or woe.

So much of a general character may be accepted without sacrificing one principle of manhood or citizen right, for that would be repugnant to our sense of absolute justice, to which we adhere without deviation or quibble.

As a fair statement of our convictions, we affirm it that there is no manhood or citizen right guaranteed to us by the Federal Constitution which which we do not claim and denial of which by State Constitutions against which we do not protest.

Passing from abstract statement of sentiment to concrete statement of fact, we have to congratulate ourselves that the race has everywhere grown stronger and stronger in all the elements of Christian morality, of thrift and intelligence. There is no contention here. Friends and foes alike admit it. Those who predicted that we should starve in a condition of freedom have lived to see us produce more and consume more than in a condition of slavery; those who prophesied that we were incapable of mastering the rudiments of education have lived to see us fill 200 colleges in the South with anxious students and to supply 25,000 competent teachers in the public schools of the South, upon whose competency white superintendents of education passed judgment; while our ignorant ministry has been transformed into one of the strongest and most intelligent forces for good in the Republic, and the high professions of law and medicine and journalism have competent representatives in every considerable community in the Republic which command the respect and confidence of their fellows.

We affirm it as a matter of fact, which cannot be refuted, that the Afro-American race is stronger and better to-day than ever before in its history; that it is more hopeful, more moral, more religious, more intelligent; that it has larger bank deposits, owns more real and personal property, and lives in better homes. As ex-Governor R. B. Bullock of Georgia recently expressed it in the New York *Sun,* no people have ever made greater progress in a given length of time.

Where it was confidently expected and predicted that we would become a dependent, pauper race in a condition of freedom, we have proved ourselves a self-sustaining race, producing more cotton and corn and other wealth as freemen to the enrichment of the commerce of the States of the South than was ever dreamed of in the philosophy of the slave-master. We appeal to the statistics of cotton and cereal and mineral production before and since the war to sustain our contention. We have not produced all the wealth of the South since the war—we have produced our honest share, produced vastly more as a freeman than we produced as a slave—and instead of becoming public charges have become self-sustaining and reliant citizens, who share in the wealth we have produced and rejoice in it and in the strength, the expansion and glory of the Republic, of which we are, as Dr. David Gregg of Brooklyn recently affirmed, among the first families, and in whose past achievements and present glory, in war and in peace, we claim by right of honest labor and sacrifice and devotion, a co-equal share and participation.

It seems to us strange and unnatural that we should have to turn from the magnificent record we have made as slaves and freemen, in peace and in war, to specific grievances which go at the very roots of our citizenship, and to appeal from the injustice and inhumanity of a portion of our fellow-citizens to the justice and fairness and Christian Charity inherent in the heart and the soul of the great American people. But we have to do so. We do it with a confidence born of Christian faith and 250 years of education in American law and precedent that we shall not appeal in vain. We have lived in darker hours than those of to-day; we have seen American justice and fair play go through fire and death and devastation and come out purified by the faith that abides in the God of Destiny, and we expect to see it do so again. Our optimism

THE AFRO-AMERICAN COUNCIL 137

is as expansive as American love of justice and fair play. And when properly appealed to, when properly aroused, we do not believe that the world can furnish a sublimer reply than it can and will give. And we do not look to one section for a response, but to all sections, and especially to the South, where we know that we have friends who have been tried in the furnace of experience and found true, and who will be faithful in the future as they have been in the past, if we shall be true to ourselves, true to the God who brought us out of Egypt of slavery into the Judea of freedom.

But no race has ever risen out of the shadows into the sunlight without fierce opposition. We have been no exception to the rule. And all the way to the top of the ladder, where Daniel Webster declared there was plenty of room, however long it takes—and time is the most important factor in the economy of God in working out the destiny of races and nations—we shall encounter fierce antagonism, but we shall win in the end, for we shall have God and justice and fair play on our side.

In view of the present condition of affairs in which we find ourselves we beg to direct attention to the following facts:

1. Since 1868 there has been a steady and persistent determination to eliminate us from the politics of the Southern States. We are not to be eliminated. Suffrage is a federal guaranty and not a privilege to be conferred or withheld by the States. We contend for the principle of manhood suffrage as the most effective safeguard of citizenship. A disfranchised citizen is a pariah in the body politic. We are not opposed to legitimate restriction of the suffrage, but we insist that restrictions shall apply alike to all citizens of all States. We are willing to accept an educational or property qualification, or both; and we contend that retroactive legislation depriving citizens of the suffrage rights is

a hardship which should be speedily passed upon by the courts. We insist that neither of these was intended or is conserved by the new constitutions of Mississippi, South Carolina or Louisiana. Their framers intended and did disfranchise a majority of their citizenship because of "race and color" and "previous condition," and we therefore call upon the Congress to reduce the representation of those States in the Congress as provided and made mandatory by Section 2 of Article XIV of the Constitution. We call upon Afro-Americans everywhere to resist by all lawful means the determination to deprive them of their suffrage rights. If it is necessary to accomplish this vital purpose to divide their vote in a given State we advise that they divide it. The shibboleth of party must give way to the shibboleth of self-preservation.

2. The increase of mob and lynch law in the Republic must be a source of regret and grief to every law-abiding citizen. It has become a source of reproach at home and abroad. We feel that this cancer on the body politic is breeding a contempt for law which will spread over the whole body of the nation unless a stop is put to it. The recent outbreaks of it in Illinois, North Carolina and South Carolina have shocked and disgusted the Nation. We regret that the President of the United States saw fit to treat with silence this vital matter in his second Annual Message to Congress, and yet we indulge the hope that the President will adjust the matter affecting the outrages in the Carolinas to the satisfaction of all fair-minded men and to the honor and glory of the Nation.

3. The separate car laws have grown to such provoking proportions, and they are so unjust, degrading and oppressive in their operations, that we deem it urgent to direct attention to them here. We urge and advise, in the interest of justice and decency, that the graduated passenger rate prevailing in North Carolina be substituted for the infamous system now in force in

THE AFRO-AMERICAN COUNCIL 139

most of the other States of the South. It is a principle of the common law that a man shall pay for what he wants and get what he pays for. Under the prevailing system a contract made in New York with a railroad or other common carrier is not worth the paper it is written on south of North Carolina. Is this fair or just. or in accordance with common or statute law practice in the United States? A contract valid in one State of the Republic should be valid in every State. With all citizens than Afro-Americans, it is.

4. In the interest of humanity we request that the penal institutions of the South be reformed. The horrors of them, depicted by Geo. W. Cable years ago, instead of growing better have grown worse, as Governor Atkinson of Georgia showed in the last days of his conscientious administration of his office. The indiscriminate herding of males and females and juveniles in the convict camps of the South constitutes one of the most glaring scandals in the administration of justice in the Republic. The horrors of Siberia as depicted by George Kennan and Stepniak are humane in comparison with these horrors within our own land. Read the reports of Governor Atkinson's special commissioners on the Georgia convict camps! And this is only one of eleven similar conditions. Separate the males from the females; give the juveniles an asylum of their own and an opportunity to reform. The other States of the Union do it, why can't the South? It has wealth enough, it only needs inclination. We appeal to its inclination. As a matter of fact there must be no less than 500,000 Afro-Americans in the Southern States who are held to involuntary service, contrary to the XIIIth Amendment to the Constitution of the United States and the peonage statutes thereof.

5. Intelligent citizenship is the strongest safeguard of the State, and as the people have decided, in the failure of the passage of the Blair Educational Bill,

that each State must tax itself to educate its own citizens, a principle entirely just, and as the taxation for school purposes in the Southern States is wholly inadequate to obliterate the abnormal illiteracy of those States—due in large part to the maintenance of separate schools for the two races, necessitating a double expenditure of moneys raised by taxation for school purposes, we suggest that a part of the public domain of each of the Southern States be devoted to the schools of higher learning and industrial training and for a more effective maintenance of the public school system of those States, for each race, share and share alike, to be controlled and apportioned to the schools by the Honorable Secretary of the Interior.

6. We feel that a more general distribution of the Afro-American race throughout the States of the Union and the new territories of the Republic, in order to reduce the congested population of the Southern States, would do much to simplify the race problem in those States, and we urge that such distribution should be encouraged in all reasonable ways. We have no sympathy whatever with the schemes of those who wish to have the race leave the United States for foreign countries. We shall remain here and fight out our destiny in the land of our fathers.

7. We favor both higher and industrial education, and are gratified at the splendid growth of the love of education manifested by the eagerness with which our people fill the avenues of education open to them.

8. We are gratified at the development of business enterprises of all sorts among us and we wish to encourage all such, as being among the strongest levers in the uplift of the race.

9. We submit our cause to the fair-minded men of our own land and of the world at large, and invoke the Divine interposition in our behalf.

XIII

GENERAL CONFERENCES

THE first General Conference of which I was a member and one of the secretaries met in Mother Zion Church, New York City, 1884. I represented the California Annual Conference.

It was at this General Conference I met for the first time that matchless orator of the race in the person of Dr. J. C. Price, founder of Livingstone College, Salisbury, N. C. A man of pleasing personality, handsome in appearance, symmetrical in form, uncompromising in attitude on all questions affecting his race. I considered him the noblest production of the A. M. E. Zion Church. It was at this same General Conference I met for the first time the eloquent G. W. Clinton and versatile J. C. Dancey. All three were young men full of life and ambition with a bright future, and each made himself felt at this great gathering.

It was at this General Conference that Bishop Hillary was deposed for immoral conduct. Considerable and helpful legislation was enacted; our divorce laws were strengthened, Children's Day inaugurated and the fifty cents general assessment was made mandatory. Quite a number of the young men of the conference were in favor of the One Dollar assessment, but were unable to get it through.

THE GENERAL CONFERENCE OF 1888

It was at this General Conference, which met at Newbern, N. C., 1888, that Dr. Price did his most effective work. It was his eloquence that won for us the day in our struggle to have the A. M. E. Zion Church to give up her position of Ultra-Conservatism and assume a progressive attitude, which it has retained ever since.

After a five days' struggle on the part of the progressives to increase our episcopal force we won, largely through the wonderful speech of Dr. Price, the finest I have ever heard him make. Dr. C. C. Petty and C. R. Harris were elected Bishops.

THE GENERAL CONFERENCE OF 1892.

At the General Conference, which met in Pittsburg, Pa., myself and I. C. Clinton were elected Bishops. (See report above.)

At this General Conference the following Commission was appointed on organic union of the Colored Branches of Methodism: Bishops C. R. Harris, C. C. Petty, A. Walters, Revs. N. J. Green, G. W. Offey, W. H. Goler, J. C. Price, M. F. Jacobs, A. J. Warner, Hon. J. C. Dancey, Rev. E. H. Curry and F. Killingsworth. The Commission met a similar commission from the A. M. E. Church at Harrisburg, Pa., May 20, 1892. They

GENERAL CONFERENCES 143

agreed on a name and bases of union, but the matter was never consummated.

Other helpful legislation was enacted.

THE GENERAL CONFERENCE OF 1896.

The General Conference of 1896 met at State Street Church, Mobile, Ala. The battle between the Conservatives and Progressives on the increase of Bishops was renewed. The Progressives won out and three Bishops were elected. Drs. G. W. Clinton, J. B. Small and J. H. Holiday were elected.

At this General Conference a strenuous effort was made by the Progressives to increase the General Funds to One Dollar per member. In this matter the Progressives failed.

The back salaries of the Bishops were stopped and they were made preferred payments on the General Funds. Our educational work was strengthened, and because of the success of the General Conference many thought that a new epoch had dawned upon the church.

WASHINGTON, 1900

At Washington a heated debate was waged on the question of increased Episcopal supervision. It resulted in the adoption of a motion providing for the election of one Bishop. Dr. J. W. Alstork of Montgomery, Alabama, was elected by acclamation. It was here that the Connectional Council was created on motion of the writer. (See General Conference Manual for 1900, page 82.)

Some notable addresses were delivered. Those by Rev. A. P. Miller, of Lincoln Memorial Church; Mr. Robert H. Terrel, Judge Gibson, Congressman from Tennessee, were pleasing and inspiring.

Remarkably clear, pungent, illuminating and suggestive was the Quadrennial Address. On racial, sociological, ecclesiastical and connectional matters it took high and advanced ground. The old church again unfurled to the breeze the banner of higher education supplemented by ministerial efficiency. On these two kindred subjects there have always been men of forward looking who constitute the vanguard. These have stood like "Stoics of the woods," contending for an educational propaganda. To-day it is evident that the rear is resting where the vanguard of yesterday camped.

ST. LOUIS, MO., 1904

Here again a titanic struggle ensued over the election of men to the high and holy office of the Bishopric. The outcome was the election of Dr. J. W. Smith, editor of the *Star of Zion*, and Dr. J. S. Caldwell, financial secretary.

It was here in the tower of the historic Washington Chapel, at the hour of midnight, when vigilant spirit was ensconced in tired flesh, that I prevailed on the senior bishop, Right Rev. J. W. Hood, to agree to the recommendation of increasing of the General Claims to one dollar per capita.

GENERAL CONFERENCES 145

Heretofore it had ranged from fifty to eighty cents. This has meant much to the progress of the church. It really marked a new epoch in our history.

PHILADELPHIA, PA., 1908

This was a General Conference of singular force and startling initiative on the part of the trenchmen, both ministerial and lay.

A struggle, fierce and absorbing, raged between the radical-progressives and the more conservative forces. The fortunes of battle favored first one and the other side. Finally, all the progressives rallied to the charge and in a brilliantly-executed flanking movement drove the conservatives from their trenches, capturing strongly defended positions, compelling a grand retreat and emerging victorious, shouting over the election of Drs. M. R. Franklin, G. L. Blackwell and A. J. Warner.

The General Conference here formulated the boards which are now in operation and made still more distinctive the several departments of the Church.

The outstanding features of this General Conference were the wave of Missionary enthusiasm which engulfed the delegates and the high pitch of religious enthusiasm, which resulted in a large contribution for the purchase of the Varick Memorial Church. The securing of this edifice was especially fitting, for in the years to come, when our children ask, "what mean ye by this building"? we can reply that it is a monument to the first Negro, who, believing in the self-reliance and ability of the Negro, launched his bark on the sea of ecclesiastical independence.

CHARLOTTE, N. C., 1912

At Charlotte the battleground was marked by the first defeat suffered by the radical-progressives since 1888. Having felt the sting of defeat for five successive times, the Conservatives rearranged their battle lines and sent wave after wave, by way of assault against the "impregnable" wall of defence constructed by the Progressives. The plan of warfare was well conceived and brilliantly executed. Day after day the lines held against repeated and determined assaults. Advance was impossible, retreat unthinkable. It became apparent that no decisive result could be achieved. A draw was inevitable. Bishop J. S. Caldwell here loomed up as the pacificator of the Church. The candidates were induced to tarry a while in the prayerful retreat of the upper room. Here they poured out strong supplications with tears. Here they finally rose on stepping stones of their suppressed ambitions and consented to retire from the race. Thus the struggle ended, or was postponed to nineteen hundred and sixteen. The prominent candidates subscribing to this compact were Drs. Geo. C. Clement, J. S. Jackson, R. B. Bruce, S. L. Corrothers, W. L. Lee, R. S. Rives and J. B. Colbert.

Little legislation was enacted here because of the time devoted to futile balloting for the elec-

GENERAL CONFERENCES

tion of chief pastors, and the defiant "No's" of the protesting delegates. The united "135" will never be forgotten. Thus the General Conference held in the Queen City of the South, thus this Conference passed into history. "God moves in a mysterious way."

LOUISVILLE, KY., 1916

Here again after the lapse of forty years came the men and women of Zion in General Conference assembled, overshadowed by the spirit of the fathers and clothed in the mantle of their proficient and valuable services. In an address delivered at Gaiety Theatre the writer thus expressed himself: "Forty years ago this very month the General Conference of our church met in this city, in the little frame church on 15th St. I was present as a boy. I sat around the altar, looked into the faces of the splendid men and women who composed that august body. At that time I never dreamed that I would be thus honored by my church as I have been, or that I would live to see such a body as is gathered here in this great city. What strides of progress in these forty years! Many problems were awaiting solution. Firm determination characterized the delegates. They had determined that for Zion they would do and for the conservation of her paramount interests they would dare. Financial irregularities had to be straightened out, and the diplomatic way in which the matters of the financial department were approached and handled speaks volumes for the sagacity and balance of the leaders of the church. Again came a gigantic struggle between the ancient rivals—progressives and conservatives—the situation was more complex than ever. To carry out their program the radical-progressives had to overcome the scruples of the conservative among them. Between them and the consummation of the things in their heart loomed up the stalwart figures of the Nestor of Zion Methodism. Retirement was recognized tacitly as the need of the hour. But the esteem in which both Bishops Hood and Harris were held made the attempt seem ludicrous and impossible. The progressives hesitated. There was perceptible faltering in their ranks. But, like the Germans at Verdun, the conservatives themselves opened the attack. In a characteristic assault on Dr. J. J. Smyer, Bishop Hood in his Episcopal address advanced to what proved to be a veritable Waterloo. The reply by Dr. Smyer will rank as a classic. The progressives then took the offensive and made a terrific onslaught on the conservatives, which resulted in the election of four Bishops.

At this General Conference Bishop Hood and Bishop C. W. Harris were retired. The financial plan was revised at this session. An assessment made of $115,000 per annum, a sufficient amount to pay off the budget of the church. The financial plan was revised appropriating 25 per cent of the General Fund or one-fourth of the amount raised. The total appropriation, $120,000.

XIV

MY TRIP TO WEST COAST OF AFRICA

> "Shall we, whose souls are lighted
> With wisdom from on high,
> Shall we to men benighted
> The lamp of life deny?"

IN accordance with the demands of my Church and in company with Bishop I. B. Scott of the M. E. Church, resident Bishop of Monrovia, Liberia, and Mr. Philip Payton, real estate dealer of New York City, I sailed on the 26th of January, 1910, for West Africa.

After a pleasant sail of seven days we reached Liverpool, England. We had to wait over for a week in order to catch a fast steamer for Monrovia. Mr. Payton remained in Liverpool two weeks awaiting the arrival of United States Minister Lyons, who he hoped would join him from America, but Mr. Payton was disappointed and had to make the journey to Monrovia alone.

Bishop Scott and I left Liverpool on the 9th of February for Monrovia. We were fortunate in securing passage on the steamer *Dakar,* one of the fastest vessels of the Elder Dempster Line.

The first five or six days of the voyage were

rather rough; on the sixth day we reached Las Palmas, and we were glad to have the opportunity to send off mail to relatives and friends in America. Las Palmas is a Spanish city of the Canary Islands. It has a healthy climate. Many English and Americans who do business in Africa have their residences in these islands.

Six days' sail from here brought us to Sierra Leone. Freetown, the chief city of the colony, is a beautiful place of 40,000 inhabitants; it is situated on the side of a mountain. Here I found black men in charge of all kinds of governmental positions. The bankers are black, the men in charge of the boats are black; all except the high government officials are colored.

It is the first great Negro city I ever saw.

There are forty churches in the city owned and controlled by black men.

LIBERIA

I left Sierra Leone on Sunday, the 20th. I was up early Monday morning, February 21, and on deck to get the first sight of Liberia. I did not have to wait very long ere I got a glimpse of the mainland, and soon we were in sight of Monrovia, the Capital of the little Black Republic, founded in 1847, colonized by free Negroes in 1821. We cast anchor about a mile from the shore, fired a signal to inform the Liberians that a vessel was in the harbor. The regular mail-boats do not stop at Monrovia, so we were not expected until the 26th of February. It was

MY TRIP TO AFRICA 151

but a short while before we saw the little boats coming out to meet us; first, the diving boys, who are experts at seeing money under water and catching it ere it reaches the bottom; next came the government officers, a fine set of young looking Negroes, as gallant looking as any set of officers I ever saw. We with our luggage were placed aboard the boats; we waved a farewell to the officers and fellow passengers of the ship, *Dakar,* and were off to shore, while the ship started to the far south. A kind of bond of friendship had sprung up between crew and passengers while aboard; hence I was a little sorry to leave them, but at last we waved the final farewell and became interested in our own skilled oarsmen. Why, what master strokes! And now we are at the wharf at Monrovia. A thrill of joy possessed me as I stepped from the boat on to the shores of my fatherland.

THE DARK CONTINENT

Africa is next in area to Asia, approaching twelve million square miles, with about two hundred million people, with an area large enough to take in Europe with her three million seven hundred and ninety-five thousand seven hundred and eighty-eight square miles; India with one million seven hundred sixty-six thousand six hundred forty-two square miles; China with one million five hundred thirty-two thousand four hundred twenty square miles; United States with three million ninety-two thousand six hundred seventy-nine square miles, all can be placed in different parts of Africa and room left for more. Africa has fifty-five million Mohammedans, one hundred million pagans and less than nine million Christians.

It has a number of diamond mines. About twenty million dollars' worth of diamonds are taken annually from the Kimberley Mines, $350,000,000 worth being the output of the uncut stones (doubled in value when cut) since 1868.

It has also a number of gold mines. A total of two hundred million dollars' worth of gold has been exported from the Gold Coast. The present annual production of gold of South Africa is fifty million dollars.

In palm oil exportation two hundred million five hundred thousand dollars was the figure reached in 1900 from the British Nigeria alone. Besides this there is a large trade in ivory and an increasing trade in rubber, mahogany, ebony, wool and other articles.

Africa's foreign commerce, exports and imports, amounted in 1901 to a grand total of seven hundred million dollars.

The continent of Africa contains some of the highest mountains in the world. The Kenia mountains have a peak 19,000 feet high.

The Ruwensori group has two peaks over 14,000 feet high. Africa has some of the greatest rivers and lakes of the world. Tanganyika Lake is 400 miles long. Lake Nyassa is about the same length. The Nile, 4000 miles long; the Congo, the Niger

MY TRIP TO AFRICA 153

and Gambesi are among the greatest rivers in the world. England, France, Germany, Portugal and Belgium are the countries which have the largest possessions in Africa.

Liberia owes its existence to the National Colonization Society of America, which was organized in 1816 for the purpose of settling in Africa the free Negroes of the United States. After an unsuccessful attempt to establish a colony south of Sierra Leone, 1820, a tract of land was acquired about Cape Mesurado. The Republic is the outgrowth of this colony.

We had a pleasant and profitable session of the conference. I was greatly assisted by Revs. Taylor and Pearce, and since it has been reported in the *Star of Zion*, I need not speak of it in detail in this address.

Sir Harry Johnston in his history of Liberia says: "Liberia is a portion of the West Coast lands between Sierra Leone and the Ivory Coast, which may be styled the end of Northern Guinea. Its most easterly point on the coast is the mouth of the Cavalla River, just beyond Cape Palmas; it is in longitude 7° 33′ W. of Greenwich; the westernmost point of Liberia (at the mouth of the River Mano) lies in about latitude 6° 55′ N., and in west longitude 11° 33′.

"In the interior Liberian territory extends northwards to about 8° 50′ N. latitude. It has three hundred miles of coast land with one or two fairly good harbors."

Sir Harry Johnston further says: "The political geography of Liberia at the present day makes it out to be a territory approximately forty-three thousand square miles in extent; bounded on the west by the British Colony of Sierra Leone, on the north and east by the French possessions in the Niger Basin and on the Ivory Coast. The southern boundary, of course, is the Atlantic Ocean.''

Liberia has four counties and one territory. The counties are Montserrado, Grand Bassa, Sinoe and Maryland; territory, Grand Cape Mount. Its principal cities are Monrovia, Robertsport, Buchanan, Edina, Greenville and Harper. The principal river is the St. Paul, a most beautiful stream, on which it was our good pleasure, through the kindness of Bishop Ferguson, to have a sail of fifteen or twenty miles out to his Girls' Industrial School, the cost of which was $30,000. Next of importance is the Cavalla, Mano, St. John, Junk and Cestos Rivers.

The principal offices of the Government are the President, Secretary of State, Secretary of the Treasury, Secretary of War and Navy, Secretary of the Interior, Postmaster General, and Superintendent of Education. Various Courts ending with the Supreme Court of three Judges. The present form of government has been in existence sixty-three years and the chief executive office has been filled by some very able men, such as Hon. J. J. Roberts, S. A. Benson, G. W. Gibson, J. J. Cheeseman and the present incumbent, President Arthur Barclay.

THE LATE TROUBLE

Because of the encroachment of France and England upon the territory of Liberia, which threatened its existence and final absorption—France having already taken a large slice of its territory—the financial embarrassment of the country, due to its inability to meet a loan advanced by an English Syndicate, decreased revenues, owing to the cheapening in price of coffee and other articles of export.

The policing of the frontiers became a great drain upon the revenues of the country—all these troubles paralyzed business and caused universal discouragement.

In the hour of this crisis it was thought wise to appeal to the Government of the United States to intervene and give financial assistance.

"That Liberia," says the Chicago *Record Herald*, "is in pressing need of a reorganization of its finances is apparent when it is considered that the British Government has been pressing for some readjustment of the situation regarding the loan, now amounting to about $455,000, including interest; the debt was incurred in 1871, through British financiers."

There is a further customs loan of $480,000 and an internal debt amounting to about $300,000.

For a population of 2,000,000 this would not seem to make a formidable grand total of indebtedness. According to reports of recent years the country has great natural resources, if they can be developed properly. How to bring about the development of these natural resources is a problem more perplexing to Liberian statesmen than is the handling of the existing indebtedness.

The *Cornhill Magazine* of June, 1890, speaking of the partitionment of Liberia among the powers mentioned, says: "The territory now known as Liberia should be divided among the powers and governed as a Protectorate in the ordinary manner unless, indeed, the United States themselves were disposed to take the whole."

"It is improbable that such a proposal would meet with serious opposition by England, France or Germany. Although it might not be exactly greeted with enthusiasm, provided that freedom of commerce were guaranteed, no differential tariffs set up and no monopoly created in Kru labor.

"Many people outside of official circles would cordially welcome the advent of the United States as an African Power. In the absence of any such professed desire on the part of the United States, the natural inheritors of the territory would be France and England, whose possessions run parallel with it.

"France would extend her Ivory Coast and Western Sudan possessions to incorporate a portion of it, and England might be disposed—the authorities of Sierra Leone would favor the course —to a further portion. Both powers, however, England especially, would be wise in making it possible for Germany to participate on equal

MY TRIP TO AFRICA

terms in the settlement, which would give her the chance, if it proved attractive in her eyes, to found in this section of Western Africa another such small Protectorate as 'Toga,' which she governed so admirably and the prosperity of whose inhabitants she has so materially increased.''

In 1908 a deputation was sent from Liberia to the United States to appeal to the Government at Washington for help, especially for intervention on the part of the United States Government. After due consideration in 1910, the Government at Washington decided to aid the black Republic through a million dollar loan from American, British, French and German bankers, through the good offices of Secretary Knox, so as to put it on a sound financial basis, which has seemed impossible of attainment. President Taft, soon after his inauguration, sent a commission of investigation to the country on the petition of the Liberians for a treaty, under which the United States, through a protectorate, might act the part of the big brother to the struggling Republic. Neither the President nor Secretary Knox, according to the advices from Washington, is in favor of an open and declared protectorate. But they hold that by the very terms of Liberia's existence the United States has a moral obligation toward the country, and cannot afford to see the struggling Negro republic gobbled up by Great Britain, France or some other European power. With a stable government and good public schools the future of Liberia is assured. Our first work is to establish a good school with an industrial department. I am convinced that if a permanent work is to be done in Africa its basis must be laid in education, and by all means Christian education. The church must be the outgrowth of the school.

On our part there must be more definite training given the men and women we purpose sending to Africa. In the past we did things in a haphazard way by sending men and women illy prepared to do this stupendous work—this must cease, and systematic efforts must be taken in its place. Men and women must be trained for work in Africa.

Liberia presents splendid opportunities for our missionary activities. (We are in a position to do as much for the country as any other colored church.) What is needed is aggressive measures and that immediately, for there is no time to be lost.

The opportunities are great for young men of training, who have a little capital and who are willing to work. Public roads, railways of all kinds are to be constructed; manufactories and steamboats are to be built; indeed, the whole country is to be opened up to commerce.

Men are needed of the highest technical training. Mr. Falkner, a young man of this country, went to Liberia and started an ice factory, built a telephone line, and he is doing well—bids fair to become one of Liberia's wealthiest citizens.

I arrived at Cape Coast, Wednesday, March

16, at 5 P.M., five days ahead of time. I had written Rev. Arthur Pinanko that my ship, according to published schedule, would arrive March 21, 1910, but catching the *Falaba* at Monrovia, March 14, I was enabled to come in on the 16th of March.

On the night of my arrival, at about 8 P.M., a delegation, consisting of the pastor, Rev. Brown, and officers of the church, called, and through an interpreter informed me that arrangements had been made to meet me at the Custom House and welcome me to the city; that a dozen or more banners had been made at great expense for the occasion; "and now," said the interpreter, "we desire your Lordship to meet the members and friends at the Custom House at 8 A.M., and allow us to escort your Lordship to your headquarters." I consented, but had to change the program next morning, owing to the fact that I did not feel well. However, the procession was formed and marched in the following order:

First Division—The day school with three banners, inscribed, "Welcome to Cape Coast"; "Search the Scriptures"; "Labore et Honore."

Second Division—The Sunday School, with three banners inscribed, "Welcome," "Feed My Lambs," and "Star of Zion; Shine on, Little Star!"

Third Division—Varick Christian Endeavor Society, with three banners inscribed, "For Christ and His Church," "Satisfy us early with Thy Mercy," and "If the Cross we bear, the Crown we will wear."

Fourth Division—Church members, with three banners inscribed, "Welcome," "God shall supply all your need," and "I will guide thee with mine eye."

The company filled the space in front of the Prospect House. It was truly an inspiring scene. Several native airs were sung to my great delight. One of the things of interest to me was to see so many people in their native dress. Presiding Elder Pinanko, on behalf of the assembly, gave a short address of welcome from the piazza of the Prospect House. In my reply I said: "I am glad to be here to meet you, and I most heartily thank you for your cordial welcome; I feel to be one of you, bone of your bone, and flesh of your flesh. I bring you greetings from the Mother Church; she wishes you great success. I congratulate you on the splendid work that you have accomplished here in the past six years, and trust it is but the beginning of a greater work for the Master. We had a splendid session of the Conference. I have heard a great deal of Cape Coast and its Castle. I have seen it for myself, and I assure you that I am delighted. I am pleased with your beautiful banners. Again God bless you all."

While in Monrovia I made my home with Hon. F. E. R. Johnson, LL.D., Secretary of State. His residence is the handsomest in the city.

MY TRIP TO AFRICA 161

REPORT OF CAPE COAST

The city of Cape Coast is about seven hundred miles from Monrovia, Liberia, and is considered the most beautiful in appearance from the sea of any of the stations on the Gold Coast. It has a population of over ten thousand. Like Rome, it is situated on seven hills. The famous Cape Coast Castle is the largest and most imposing of the many castles along the West Coast of Africa, and has an interesting history. I was surprised to see so many beautiful public buildings and fine private dwellings here.

Our school building, which is being used for Church services, will accommodate five or six hundred. It is built with cement and it presents a clean and healthful appearance. I had no idea that we had such a large and substantial building in Africa.

As usual, our ship anchored about a half mile from the shore, and I was again forced, against my will, to take a small boat for the land. We had ten boys set on the edge of the boat, and how they did sing and paddle as our boat rode the mighty waves.

There is no wharf or dock at Cape Coast to which even the little boats can tie up, so when we got as near land as possible, two strong fellows took me on their shoulders and carried me to shore—how I did rejoice that I had made the journey safely. It was soon known that the African Bishop from America had arrived. I sent for Rev. Arthur Pinanko, but ere he arrived some female members of the mission came and took my luggage on their heads (where everything is carried from a cup to an iron bar weighing a ton) and started for the Parsonage. I had fourteen pieces of luggage, which furnished the opportunity for quite a procession. We had hardly gotten out of the gate of the Custom House before I met two of our preachers, Brothers Brown and Sackay, and soon afterward saw the smiling face of Rev. Arthur Pinanko rushing to meet me. My, but I was glad to see him. Had he been a woman I would have kissed him. He led the procession to the Parsonage, which is a fine building in a good locality. I was informed that I was to rest a while there; that headquarters had been arranged at a place on one of the Hills of Cape Coast—Prospect House. I had never occupied in America such a place. The position of the building is a commanding one—away above the houses in the valley. On three sides is a splendid view of the ocean and on the north a view far back into the hinderland. This is the property we hope to secure for our College. Rev. Pinanko and his wife were with me and we had servants galore. How I wish all our Bishops could visit this place and see this situation—meet these grandees. The men are tall, straight as an arrow, symmetrical in form, comely in appearance; for a head dress they coil a handkerchief with different colors round their heads; they wear a cloth one side thrown over the shoulder coming

MY TRIP TO AFRICA 163

down to about a foot of the ground; the well-to-do wear sandals, but the majority go barefooted. The women wear a piece of cloth from the breast down to about half a foot from the ground. I was agreeably surprised with the modest style of the dress of the young women. The little children wear very little clothes, some of them none at all. The professional and the merchant class are Europeanized; they dress very much like the English or the American, but they form the small minority.

The whole Gold Coast is under the English rule, with a Governor at Accra, and a Deputy Governor (Commissioner) at Cape Coast. Still, the local King Kodwo Morah is in charge of the natives. He is the first black King that I ever saw. It was my pleasure to meet him twice, and I consider him a fine old man. He is over ninety years old. He was present at my reception at Cape Coast and made an address. Chief W. Z. Coker, commander (General) of the warriors, is a colored man. He delivered the welcome address on behalf of the City—at our reception.

KWITTAH

I left Cape Coast on March 28 for Kwittah, our last station on the West Coast of Africa, in company with Presiding Elder Frank Pinanko and Rev. Harold N. Kwaun, a delegate from Kwittah to the Conference held at Cape Coast. We arrived Wednesday, March 30, 1910, and were met at the shore by Rev. W. E. Shaw and J. D. Taylor; the latter and his wife preceded me here from Monrovia by twelve days. A special boat was sent out to our ship to convey us to the land.

The church, school and citizens with beautiful banners were on hand to escort us to the parsonage; most of the people were in their native dress. On all sides could be seen flags with the word Welcome inscribed on them. It was truly a royal welcome. The scene was an inspiring one not soon to be forgotten by me.

I found Rev. Shaw in perfect health and as happy as it is possible to be. He seems delighted with his work, and the people are exceedingly pleased with him. In the short time he has been there he has transformed things, both in the church and school. We have a very good school building, 40 by 60, which we use for church services. I am told that it is usually filled each Sabbath. A short distance from Kwittah, at Payie, we have here a young Tuskegee, organized by Rev. J. J. Pearce. I am told that it is a great plant. Rev. Shaw has promised to send to the *Star* a full account of this remarkable work.

Kwittah is a town of ten thousand inhabitants on a plain; unlike Cape Coast, seated on seven hills. It is a clean city with fine private and public buildings.

Considerable cotton is raised near here. The chief planter is Mr. Dawson, a member of our church. He is intelligent, thrifty, and a public-spirited young man. I feel proud of him and of

MY TRIP TO AFRICA

his achievements. He presented me two pillows made of the cotton grown on his place.

The first session of the East Gold Coast Conference of the A. M. E. Zion Church convened at Kwittah, Thursday, March 31, at 10 A.M., with five ministers and nine lay delegates present. Rev. Harold N. Kwaun was chosen secretary and Presiding Elder Shaw compiler and reporter to the *Star of Zion*.

On Thursday night, March 30, Welcome exercises were held at the school building. The place was packed and there were as many on the outside as there were within. Able addresses were made by the secretary of the trustee board, Revs. Arthur Pinanko, J. D. Taylor and W. E. Shaw. I made a response.

The sessions of the Conferences were interesting. Brother Harold N. Kwaun and G. A. Tay were ordained deacons and three other young men of our teaching force were admitted to the Conference. The Conference settled an old dispute about the land which is in our charge. It was given to the connection by Chief Acolatse. It was afterwards discovered that he did not own all the land included in the deeds given us, but that a part of the land was owned by Chief Ocloo. During a visit here of Rev. Pinanko to settle the matter Chief Ocloo agreed to give a deed for his part of the land, and since the land had been properly surveyed and Chief Acolatse was willing to make another deed, the matter was settled without much trouble.

Splendid sermons were preached during the Conference by Revs. Pinanko, Taylor and Shaw. Of course, the Bishop had to preach.

On Thursday, Friday and Saturday nights and Sunday hundreds came forward for prayer. I never saw anything like it in my life. Forty joined the church and as many were baptised. We have a membership here of over three hundred, and in the day school we have two hundred and seventy scholars, with seven instructors. The following is the report of our work here at Kwittah. If our great Bishop Small was alive, who laid the foundation of this work, how his heart would rejoice, and I dare to think that he does know of the work, and that he does rejoice at the wonderful progress made. Bishop Small built wiser than he knew.

The important question with our Church to-day is, shall we commence a more aggressive work in Africa? This question can best be answered by asking another—are we prepared to do aggressive work in Africa? I answer unhesitatingly, yes. Since its origin the Zion Church has been known for its independence—race pride and true patriotism. No Negro Church has produced a greater galaxy of heroic leaders than the A. M. E. Zion Church. When the future historian shall make up his roll of honor of the Negro leaders of America in the Church, high on that scroll will appear the names of James Varick, Christopher Rush, Jackson J. Clinton, John Jamison Moore, J. W. Loguen, Singleton T. Jones, Calvin Petty,

MY TRIP TO AFRICA

Frederick Douglass, J. B. Small, William Howard Day, Joseph C. Price, J. W. Hood and J. C. Dancey.

In the dark days of slavery when a platform was needed for the Negro to plead his own cause, notwithstanding the threatening of slave-holders and their sympathizers in the North and South, Zion Church gave to the anti-slavery advocates a platform. The very genius of the Church is one of independence. There is not a Bishop alive to-day who is not filled with an aggressive spirit and who is not manly and courageous. I know the men of my Church, and no matter what men may say and think to the contrary, they are for the noblest and best there is for their race, and this is the spirit they are prepared to carry into Africa.

SECOND.—HAS THE A. M. E. ZION CHURCH MEN AND WOMEN QUALIFIED TO DO EFFECTIVE WORK IN AFRICA?

Again I answer in the affirmative. We have in our ranks men from some of the best schools in the nation. Not long ago we sent to Africa a man eminently prepared by literary training and experience to give splendid service in the redemption of that dark continent. He is a trained physician, Rev. W. E. Shaw. At Cape Coast we have in the person of Frank Arthur a man trained in our own Livingstone, a person of deep Christian piety. At Brewerville we have Rev. J. J. Pearce of Fiske University, a man not only of training, but of experience and in every way prepared to advance the work. At Monrovia we have J. D. Taylor, the dean of our missionary corps in Africa.

Doubtless there are many in our own schools to-day that are being prepared for service in Africa. Thus we see that from an intellectual standpoint our Church is prepared to do effective work in Africa.

THIRD.—HAS THE A. M. E. ZION CHURCH THE MONEY SUFFICIENT TO CARRY ON THE WORK IN AFRICA?

Again we say yes. We have the same kind of people and with just about as much money as any other Negro Church in America. If the A. M. E. Church can carry on work in Africa so can we.

I have nothing but words of commendation for this great Church and its work in Africa. I rejoice in the fact that Bishops Turner, Grant, Smith, Derrick and Coppin have visited that far-off land, touched and inspired its people. I am glad that Bishop Heard is the resident Bishop of Liberia and that Bishop Johnson is the resident Bishop of South Africa. And I am sorry that we have not done as much, and I serve notice to-day that Zion is alive to the missionary interest of Africa, and from now on proposes to be an active factor in the redemption of that land.

I rejoice in the splendid work done by the Baptist Churches of Color in the redemption of Africa. They have done and are doing a magnificent work, and I believe that we are as well prepared as they are, according to our numbers, to do effective work in Africa.

All admit that the world must be converted to God, and the A. M. E. Zion Church must do its part or else prove recreant to its trust. The Church that is foremost in the missionary endeavor will be the Church to receive the largest blessing from God, for the promise is to those who will spread the word of God and teach all nations.

To do this the first requisite is an experimental knowledge of Jesus Christ the Lord, and in proportion as this is genuine and deep will we desire to communicate His fire to others. The same is true of the Church. Propagation is the law of the natural world. When we have a delightful experience we feel like making it known to others, so when we have the gift of the Holy Ghost and know of the love of God, we must communicate it to others.

"People who say that they do not believe in foreign missions are usually quite unconscious of the indictment which they bring against their own spiritual experience. The man that has no religion of his own that he values, of course is not interested in the effort to make it known to others. One may simply be ignorant of the contents of his faith or the real character of the missionary movement, but as a rule those who have the real Christian experience are conscious of an overmastering impulse to communicate it to others."

When Andrew had found the Christ had come in

touch with His charming personality, had listened to His burning words of eloquence and had been mightily wrought upon by His wonderful love, he ran off to inform his brother Simon, and said to him, "We have found the Messiah." The woman of Samaria who conversed with Christ at Jacob's well became enthused over the words of the Master, and finally returned to the village of Sychar and said, "Come see a man which told me all the things whatever I did; is not this the Christ"? The four men who forcibly carried the leper into the presence of Jesus did so because they had themselves been healed of their maladies.

THE WORLD'S NEED OF CHRIST

In setting forth the needs of the world, St. Paul has declared: "We have all gone astray, sinned and fallen short of the glory of God." Isaiah declared: "The whole world is sick and the heart faint, from the sole of the foot even to the head, there is no soundness in us, wounds and bruises and putrefying sores."

If such is the condition with enlightened people, how much more are the heathens in need of the Saviour, who are without enlightenment.

Says Rev. Arthur Brown: "He who has knowledge that is essential to his fellowmen is under obligation to convey that knowledge to them." It makes no difference who those men are or where they live, or whether they are conscious of their need, or how much inconvenience or expense he may incur in reaching them; the fact that he can help them is the reason why he should help them. This is an essential part of the foreign missionary impulse. We have the revelation of God which is potential of a civilization that benefits man; an education that fits him for higher usefulness, a scientific knowledge that enlarges his power, a medical skill that alleviates his suffering, and above all, a relation of Jesus Christ that not only lends a new dignity to his earthly life, but that saves his soul and prepares him for eternal companionship with God. "In none other is there salvation." Therefore, we must convey this gospel to the world. There is no worthy reason for being concerned about the salvation of the man next to us which is not equally applicable to the man five thousand miles away."

The imperative command, "Go ye therefore, and teach all nations"; the little word "go" in the sentence just quoted may be applied to us all, not only to the minister in the pulpit, the young man or woman in our schools having a course of preparation for the mission work, but to us all. Some of us are to go in person to the yet far-off mission fields, they are to labor in word and doctrine, to suffer for the Master. Others are to go by giving their means, and in order to do this make sacrifices to carry out the commission; and still others go by earnest and prevailing prayers for the mission cause. While we have accomplished much, still, it must be apparent to all that we could have done a great deal more.

My main object is to have our men help to civilize and Christianize heathen Africa, and this must be done quickly or Mohammedanism will overrun the country. The question is, which will conquer Africa—Islam or Christianity? Some very intelligent people think that Islam is better for Africa as a religion than Christianity, since it so completely emphasizes and practices the fatherhood of God and the brotherhood of man.

They say the Christian religion teaches the fatherhood of God and the brotherhood of man, but the white missionary studiously avoids it in practice. I am sorry this is true, but this does not destroy the fact that the Christian religion is the best in the world.

Mohammedanism encourages polygamy, which means the destruction of the home. Christianity stands for purity, which means the stability of the home and the nation. Now is the time for the Christian world to awake to the seriousness of this conflict and do all in its power to win Africa. I do think, however, that there is a great need of the principles of true Christianity everywhere: *God's purpose in allowing the natives to be brought to these shores.*

For what other purpose were the natives brought to America and caused to pass through the crucible of slavery and now to be Christianized and trained in the best schools of the nation but to aid in the redemption of Africa. More em-

MY TRIP TO AFRICA 173

phasis should be placed in such meetings as this on the part the American Negro should take in the evangelization of Africa.

Out of our meagre means we are doing what we can to establish schools to prepare missionaries for this work, and I am glad to say that a number of the white boards of America and Europe have opened the doors of their schools to admit men to be prepared for this work. But money is needed to establish schools on the grounds for the training of native workers, and I appeal to you to-day to aid us in the establishment of educational institutions.

MATERIAL DEVELOPMENT OF AFRICA

I am of the opinion that our Church should give all the encouragement possible to the material development of Africa, and especially of Liberia. I believe that America is to furnish the Negro Cecil Rhodes to Liberia, the man who is to develop the resources of Africa and to start a line of steamships between that country and ours. Untold wealth and glory await such a financial genius.

I am of the opinion that the Negroes of America should lend their influence to help in the political development of Liberia. The men who compose this historic Republic are our brothers, bone of our bone and flesh of our flesh. Therefore, they have a right to expect encouragement from us.

OUR CONTRIBUTION TO AFRICA

While Scotland can boast of her David Livingstone, who stands at the head of all African explorers; indeed, who is majestic in his loneliness and was so lofty in his purpose, so superb in his devotion, and who said when dying, "All that I can add to my loneliness is, may heaven's richest blessing come down on every one—American, Englishman, Turk—who will help heal this open sore of the world." And while the Methodist Episcopal Church can boast of her Melville Cox, who was so able and saintly, and who laid down his life for Africa's redemption, our Zion can boast of her rugged old hero, Andrew Cartright; Dudley, Mesdames Arthur and Wright; nor can we forget their services, who are the connecting links between our Church and Africa. Their departed spirits whisper to us and urge us on to play our parts in the redemption of this great continent.

All honor to Bishop Small, my predecessor, who felt the burden of African redemption as no other man felt it in his day in our Church. I am afraid that there is not enough said about the work of Bishop Small; what we have in Africa to-day is largely due to the efforts in the interest of Africa by this sainted hero.

It is known to a good many of us that out of his own private purse he aided Frank Arthur and other African students who matriculated at Livingstone College. Several of them he kept in his home, providing liberally for their physical needs. I consider it an honor to succeed such an eminent scholar, such an enthusiastic advocate of African redemption.

And now may I add to this closing word, I do hope that our Church will rise to the present situation and meet the present opportunity which is presented to it in Africa.

"If the situation now confronting the Church throughout the world does not move to a larger consecration and prompt an aggressive effort, it is difficult to imagine what more God could do to move the Church, unless it be to bring upon it some great calamity. To know the awful needs of the non-christian world, to have available a Gospel abundantly sufficient to meet that need, to be fully able to carry that Gospel to those who are in need of it, and not to do so, will inevitably promote unreality and hypocrisy throughout the Home Church. It is an inexorable law of Christianity that no Christian can keep spiritual life and blessing to himself, but must communicate to those in need. Not to do so damages the character of the Christian himself, promotes like hypocrisy among other Christians who are influenced by him, leads unbelievers around him to lose confidence in the reality of Christianity and leaves in outer darkness multitudes of souls in non-christian lands who, were it not for such sham profession, would be ushered into the marvellous light and liberty of Christ. The present halting and seeming inaction of the Church is bringing discredit on the name and power of Christianity."

Let us up and be doing. Every member of the Church and race should make an annual subscription to our African Fund. It is a shame the little we give to Foreign Missions. Who will be the first to hand in his name for an annual subscription to this fund?

XV

INDEPENDENCE IN POLITICS

"He serves me most who serves his country best."
—POPE.
"But while
I breathe Heaven's air, and Heaven looks down on me,
And smiles at my best meanings, I remain
Master of mine own self and mine own soul."
—TENNYSON.

GREATLY to the surprise of my lifelong friends and to the consternation of the conservative members of my race in politics, both in the campaign of 1908 and again in 1912, I not only voted the Democratic ticket, but took an active part in the campaign for the election of the national Democratic ticket. Much censure was bestowed upon me, both privately and publicly, for thus deserting the party to which the colored man by tradition and general consent of both the great political parties considered himself bound. In response to the publicly expressed criticism, I issued the following defence of my independence in politics, being at this time President of the Colored Democratic League:

REASONS WHY THE NEGRO SHOULD VOTE THE DEMOCRATIC TICKET

In advocating a division of the Negro vote I have met with severe criticism from some people who ought to know better. However, much of the criticism is the result of selfishness; it is the same old cry heard in other days, "Our raft is in danger."

Since I have nothing but the good of my people at heart, I have nothing to fear nor need I be disturbed by the unjust criticism so freely indulged in in some quarters.

It has been said that I desire all the Negroes to vote the Democratic ticket. I want nothing of the kind, nor have I ever by speech, letter or otherwise advised such a course; we would be as bad off politically as we are now if all the Negroes entitled to the franchise were to go over to the Democratic Party.

Our present political ills have largely come through the solidarity of the Negro vote.

PRINCIPLES OF DEMOCRACY

If Democracy stands for anything at all, it stands for the brotherhood of man, and the rule of the people. And the principles of Democracy will triumph ultimately. It is the light in our Republic that is to shine more and more unto the perfect day. Its growth is continuous.

The Negro being a member of this great Republic will be a recipient of its blessings.

Gov. Folk of Missouri says: "Democracy would have all unite in enforcing the laws and in counteracting any attempt to defy them. It would not array class against class, but would protect the rights of all by having each respect the rights of the other.

"It would not attack wealth honestly acquired, but would wage unending war against the privileges that

NEW CHURCH TO WHICH BISHOP WALTERS CONTRIBUTED THE FIRST $25

INDEPENDENCE IN POLITICS 179

produce tainted riches on one side, and undeserved poverty on the other side.

"It would protect property rights, but would recognize that property rights are best protected by preserving inviolate the public rights.

"It would not combat men but the evil men do. It would seek as a remedy for existing evils not less government by the people, but more government by the people.

"It would place conscience above cunning and the public good above private greed. It would not offer a man an advantage, in the way of subsidy, or bounty, or protective tariff, enabling him to make money at the expense of his fellow men, but it would assure him that it would give no one else such a special privilege over him.

"It would guarantee to all an equal opportunity to live and labor and enjoy the gains of honest toil."

I admit that so far as the Negro is concerned the Democratic Party has not lived up to its high principles.

Human slavery has been the great stumbling block for which the Democratic Party was not wholly responsible. Long, long before any Democratic party was formed in this country, slavery existed here, and it was the economic value of the slave that caused the perpetuity of the institution.

The Southern climate, so much like the native habitat of the African, was suited to him and he to it; it responded to his touch, producing in abundance cotton, tobacco, rice, sugar cane, etc.

He lived, thrived and made the Southland blossom like a rose.

He was considered a necessity and schemes were devised to enslave him for ever. Neither Federalists, Democrats, Whigs nor Republicans were responsible for its beginning, but rather the rulers of England, who permitted the slave trade, thus enriching themselves.

For a time slavery existed both North and South—

the cold climate of the North made slavery unprofitable in that section, while the Southern States formed a suitable field for slave labor in the production of its staple products.

With this discovery came the defence of the system. And on and on it went until the system was hedged about with laws enacted by State Legislature and the National Congress.

Next came the agitation against slavery by those who perceived the iniquity of the institution and that slavery was a menace to the continuation of the Republic.

The next act in the drama was the Civil War, which resulted in the overthrow of the system. The party which accomplished this wonderful feat was the party of Lincoln, Seward, Sumner, Stevens, Grant and others —the Republican Party.

THE NEW ADJUSTMENT

The Republican Party having freed the slaves, there was nothing else for it to do but to make them secure in their freedom; this was done by the passage of the Thirteenth Amendment to the Federal Constitution, which reads as follows:

Section 1: "Neither slavery nor involuntary servitude, except as a punishment for crime whereof the party shall have been duly convicted, shall exist in the United States, or in any place subject to their jurisdiction."

The wise statesmen who had led the party so far in legislation in the interest of the black man saw that it was necessary to go a step further and make the Negro a full-fledged citizen; this was accomplished by the passage of the Fourteenth and Fifteenth Amendments to the Federal Constitution, which reads as follows:

Section 1: "All persons born and naturalized in the United States and subject to the jurisdiction thereof, are citizens of the United States, and the State wherein they reside. No State shall make or enforce any laws which shall abridge the privileges or immunities of any citizen of the United States; nor shall any State deprive any person of life, liberty or property, without due process of the law, nor deny to any person within its jurisdiction the equal protection of its laws."

Section 2: "Representatives shall be apportioned among the several States accorded to their respective numbers, counting the whole number of persons in each State, excluding Indians not taxed; but whenever the right to vote at any election for the choice of electors for President and Vice-President of the United States, representatives in Congress, the executive and judicial officers of the State or members of the legislature thereof, is denied to any of the male inhabitants of such State, being twenty-one years of age and citizens of the United States, or in any way abridged, except for participating in rebellion or other crime, the basis of representation therein shall be reduced in the proportion which the number of such male citizens shall bear to the whole number of male citizens, twenty-one years of age in such State."

The Fifteenth Amendment reads as follows:

Section 1. "The rights of citizens of the United States to vote shall not be denied or abridged by the United States or by any State on account of race, color or previous condition of servitude."

As was expected, the South opposed this legislation; its training and tradition were all against the political equality of the black man and it found it difficult to adjust itself to the new condition. Notwithstanding the opposition the good work continued—public and private schools were established, and the black man encouraged to protect himself by the use of the ballot.

I might add here in support of the enfranchisement of the freedman that a voteless citizen is a greatly handicapped one—a pariah in the community; especially is this true when such a citizen is a member of a weaker race.

This state of affairs continued until 1876, when a change came about—the Republicans had nominated Rutherford B. Hayes, of Ohio, for the Presidency and the Democratic party had nominated Samuel J. Tilden, of New York, for the same office—the election was in doubt and it was finally settled by a commission of fifteen—five Justices of the Supreme Court, five Senators and five members from the House of Representatives.

The dispute was settled in favor of Rutherford B. Hayes and he was declared President of the United States.

It was asserted that a deal had been made between the North and the South by which President Hayes was to withdraw the troops from the South, permitting home rule to obtain.

The Negroes were loud in their protest against the dicker; they saw in it great sorrow and tribulation to the freedmen. The Federal troops in the South had been their protection and guarantee in the use of the ballot, etc., their removal meant the overthrow of the Republican administration in the South. It was the beginning of the end of the Republican rule in the lately enfranchised States.

Viewing it from this distance, it was the best thing that could have been done under the circumstances; while it was true that this act entailed hardships upon the Negro for a while, it was the only way to bring about a readjustment of affairs which would lead finally to the permanent enfranchisement of the race.

The intelligence, wealth and influence were with the white people of that section and coercion could not last forever.

Things were in a chaotic state for a while, Ku-Kluxism was rampant; but gradually this state of things passed away, and when lynchings shall have been a thing of the past, the last vestige of this régime shall have disappeared.

INDEPENDENCE IN POLITICS

It came our turn to protest against restrictive legislation such as the curtailment of political power, the nullification of the War Amendments, the introduction of Jim Crow Laws, etc.

The Republican Party had gone as far as it thought it wise to go in the way of legislation; hence it looked on with indifference while the Negro was being stripped of the privileges and immunities which the Grand Old Party had given him.

CHANGED ATTITUDE OF THE REPUBLICANS

The great champions of human liberty who had found the Republican Party had either died, left it or become a silent minority. Lincoln, Greeley and Sumner were dead.

The death of Stevens in 1868, and Sumner in 1874, left the radicals without a leader, and amidst the clamor for amnesty and general forgiveness the radical element was totally eliminated as a factor of the Republican Party.

The last radical act that Congress ever passed on the Negro question was the Civil Rights Bill, enacted as a compliment to the immortal Sumner, then dead, and which was afterward declared unconstitutional by a Republican Supreme Court.

THE REPUBLICAN PARTY STEADILY DRIFTING

Since 1880 the Republican Party has steadily drifted away from its humanitarian principle, for which, in the popular mind, it is supposed to have stood.

For thirty years the Grand Old Party has not only been permitting, but it has actually encouraged, the nullification of all the radical legislation for which it was held responsible.

It has ceased to make the Negro question a party issue—in this respect the Republican and the Democratic party are one and the same.

The Republican Party has not only stood by and seen the Negroes of the South deprived of their rights as citizens, but for the past decade has been actually engaged in the construction of a party organization in that section that stands for the elimination of the colored man in politics. This is evidenced by the position taken by ex-President Roosevelt in his late pronunciamento on the Negro question. The dullest mind can see at a glance the difference between the party as represented by Charles Sumner in 1870 and Theodore Roosevelt and William Howard Taft in 1912.

The thinking Negroes who understand the trend of things see that if the inimical legislation enacted against the Negro is to be repealed it must be done by the Democratic Party, which is now willing to accept the Negro vote and guarantee it a fair deal.

NEW ADJUSTMENT BY DEMOCRATS

The American Republic can never be an ideal one while some of its native born and worthy citizens are denied the political rights guaranteed them by the Constitution.

The tendency of the age is toward Democracy—true Democracy, the Democracy that recognizes no color nor creed, but worth only.

This leaven is at work and is as sure to result in the political emancipation of the black man as the sun shines.

The late Justice Brewer said: "The Negro will surely come into possession of the franchise in all sections of the country."

Mr. Henry Watterson, editor of the *Courier-Journal*, Louisville, Ky., and one of the foremost leaders of the Democratic Party, in fact its oracle, says: "A new generation of blacks has come upon the scene and they will finally be allowed their political rights."

A distinguished Democrat said the other day: "The Democratic party is prepared to give to the black man

INDEPENDENCE IN POLITICS 185

all he merits." The Negro is in possession of intelligence, property and character; surely these entitle him to the ballot.

Congressman Sulzer of New York, in a letter said: "Equal rights to all and special privileges to none is the fundamental principle of Democracy, and the application of this principle to questions as they arise will solve them all in the interest of the plain people of our country; it seems to me it should be the constant effort of the men of your race, in season and out of season, to keep this great principle to the front, so that all the people, without regard to race, religion or previous condition, shall be equal before the law; and the door of opportunity under the star of hope of free America ever remain open. The sentiment in favor of this idea is growing apace throughout the country and means much for the future welfare of America. Democracy has no prejudice against any race, but wants to help all sorts and conditions of people to rise step by step to higher levels in the onward march of civilization."

If time would but permit I could give lengthy quotations from leaders of the Democratic Party in the North and in the South who declare that the time has come that the party is willing to treat with the black man.

A FREED CONSCIENCE

By education, material advancement and political independence the Negro has reached the place where the right-thinking, fair-minded white men of the South are willing to accord to him his political rights, and many see the necessity of so doing if the highest ideals of this Republic are to be realized.

With a division of the Negro vote the so-called black menace will be removed and the conscientious white Democrat of the South can look his industrious, intelligent and honest black neighbor squarely in the eye with the knowledge and satisfaction that he has not denied to him any of his rights, but on the contrary has made it possible for him to cast his ballot unmolested.

With a division of the black vote we will have political friends in both parties.

AN ERRONEOUS IDEA

It has been said that when the Democratic Party gets into power that disfranchisement of the Negro would be made universal throughout the Nation. I do not believe a word of it. In order to do this, the Fifteenth Amendment would have to be repealed and this would require a three-fourths vote of all the States in the Union, and, because of the many things involved in such an action, this impregnable rock will not be removed should the government of the country be passed next year to the Democratic Party.

This argument is a cunningly devised piece of sophistry to deceive the unwary for the purpose of keeping a few office-holders in office, but which in the end will keep our people longer in political bondage.

AN INVITATION

Much is being said about the Democratic Party not wanting the vote of the Negro. This is true of the radical element in both parties. We all know that in the convention held of late by Republicans, in most of the Southern States the Negroes have been shut out. The last Negro has been put off the Republican National Committee. It will be seen by such actions that the Republicans do not want the Negro either, only as the Negro is useful to them. We have been of no use to the Democrats politically, and hence they have had nothing for us to do. There is an element in both parties that gladly welcomes the black man.

Again Mr. Watterson says: "A new generation of blacks has come upon the scene. These blacks are better educated. In the North they understand the situation. What do they owe the Republicans? In my opinion, nothing. If they ever expect to help their brethren in the South, this is a good chance to do it, because to the white people in the South they must look for substantial help and real advantage, and everything which allays race prejudice and brings the two people nearer together in friendly and neighborly intercourse will inure to the profit of the weaker in the life struggle. The *Courier-Journal* has never sought to make a party profit out of the Negro. It is his friend and his neighbor, his fellow citizen, and his fellow Christian. The whites cannot prosper if the blacks languish. We are, whites and blacks, in the same boat, and we must sit fair and row steady if we expect to be happy and make progress.

"The white man should want nothing of the benefits of government for himself and his children which he is not willing to allow the black man for himself and his children. We are mutually dependent. We are bound to live together, we cannot get away from one another, hence a good working and living understanding is the basis of the common interest.

"The black people long ago learned that the Republican Party had no use for them except to vote them. Through forty years they have been paying a debt but half owed. In the meantime the whites of the South have been aiding them in substantial ways. If they should turn about now and vote the Democratic ticket in the North, or divide their vote, they would be pursuing a wise policy by rebuking the Republicans, making fair weather with the Democrats, and asserting at once their intelligence and their independence."

The Columbia *State* of South Carolina opens its doors and invites us in and says in doing so it follows the advice of Alexander Stephens, General Gordon, Senator Zeb Vance and Matt Ransom of North Carolina, and others. There is nothing new or strange in the opposition we are meeting with in our effort to ally ourselves with the Democratic Party. We have always met with strong opposition in our endeavors to better our condition. When the Negro asked for admission into the army at the beginning of the Civil War, he was told that he was not wanted, that it was a white man's war. Even the great Lincoln, at first, threw his weight against allowing the Negro to fight, bleed and die to save the Union, and break the shackle from his own ankles and wrists. Did the Negro give up because he was not wanted?

No. He was told that he was making a fool of himself to offer himself to the Nation, to enter the army, to die to help a people who did not want him. He was driven like a dog from the Union camp, but the Negro had sense enough to know that he would better his condition by being admitted to the army, allowed to fight for his country, and his freedom, so he persisted in his efforts and he was admitted, and what a boon has come to him!

We know that we will better our condition if we finally get a permanent foothold politically in the South by allying ourselves with the Democrats, and this is the only way we are going to do it.

The old master class is too proud to take the initiative, and we need not wait for an invitation on a silver platter. Had we waited for an invitation into the army we would have been waiting until now, and if we wait to be invited by all its leaders into the Democratic Party we will have to wait a long time. No, no; we must so act to induce that party to open the door and let us in, because we will be useful to them as well as help ourselves.

REPUBLICAN PARTY INDIFFERENT TO THE RACE AND INDORSES LILYWHITEISM

The Republican Party has shown itself impotent to enact further legislation in our interest. This is evident by its failure to have Congress pass a bill to have lynchers tried in the Federal Courts. Nor has the Republican Party done anything to prevent hostile legislation on the part of the Southern States, enacted against us chiefly because we, as a race, have voted solidly with the Republican Party.

The Negro has been the ally of the Republican Party for nearly a half century; he has been cuffed and kicked about because of his loyalty to that party; especially is this true of the Southland, and the G. O. P. has looked on with indifference and has not lifted a finger to correct the evil.

We have prayed and we have made appeal after appeal to a Republican Congress for relief, only to be told that we had made our appeal to the wrong place; that we should go to the Supreme Court for redress; but when we knocked at the door of the Supreme Court and asked for relief, we were told to go back to Congress; that the matter was out of the jurisdiction of the court. Thus we have been sent by the President to the Court, from the Court to Congress, and from Congress back to the Court, and relief is about as near in sight as when we started. This but shows the impotency and unwillingness of the Republican Party to give the Negro the desired relief.

PRESIDENT TAFT'S BID FOR SUPPORT OF THE SOUTH

Ever since his election, President Taft has been flirting with the Democrats; first by the appointment of a Democrat to his cabinet and later by the appointment of a Democrat Chief Justice of the Supreme Court of the United States, and to other offices Democrats galore. Yet in the face of all this, it is considered an unpardonable sin for a Negro to affiliate with the Democratic Party, from which this man was taken and exalted by a Republican President. I have no objection to this; all I want is an opportunity to make friends with the same people.

THE NEGRO NATURALLY A DEMOCRAT

The Negro is naturally a Democrat and with an open political door and all unfavorable restriction removed, the South would soon see on which side the Negro would vote.

Politically, the attitude heretofore of the South has been such a hostile one towards the Negro that he found it utterly impossible to vote the Democratic ticket. It is hard to support a party that is continually striking you hard blows in the face by enacting laws to humiliate you and doing but little, if anything, to stop outrages perpetrated against you because of your color.

But since all of this is changing and we behold a rift in the clouds and a slow but surely rising tide of favorable sentiment to the Negro in the South, it is our duty to hail it, to fix the price the producer or farmer is to receive for his stuff. A majority of us are farmers; and ought to vote for and encourage the Democratic Party.

I appeal to that class of Democrats who are still hostile to the political aspirations of the Negro to put aside their prejudices, stop trying to disfranchise us, as has been done in Maryland again and again, and give us a chance to help you into national power. The wise men of both parties declare that the qualified Negro is sure eventually to be allowed the ballot. Why not accept his help now? He is the best friend the South has ever had or will have, outside of the native white Americans.

THE NEGRO AND THE GREAT POLITICAL ISSUES

On the great questions of tariff and the curbing of trusts, the interest of the Negroes is on the Democratic side.

It is considered that most farmers and producers of raw material are against a high tariff, because a high

INDEPENDENCE IN POLITICS

tariff means a restricted market. And while a restricted market is bad enough, the situation becomes particularly grave when combinations and cliques of manufacturers and capitalists may corner markets and manipulate affairs so as to enable them a continuance of a high tariff. Even if the mechanic and the mill hand feel the effects of the tariff on their wages, the Negro who is shut out from factory and mill is affected but remotely, if at all.

But what of the control of these trusts and combinations which have resulted from high tariff? To those who reason that these combinations or monopolies are bad whether connected with the tariff or not, and conceding that they have grown up and flourished under Republican Administrations, must be inclined to put more faith in the promise of Democrats to correct the evil than in Republicans, under whose régime trusts have sprung up and flourished. Only one has to consider whether or not trusts are undesirable and bad, and there seems to be but one opinion as to this, both Republicans and Democrats agreeing that they are harmful and vicious. Everybody remembers how rapidly trusts multiplied immediately after the election of McKinley, in 1896; practically every important industry in the country went into or formed some sort of trust within a year after November, 1896.

The Republican Party, then, is directly and absolutely responsible for these evils. Year after year this party has been put into power; it has had the chance to prevent the conditions now complained of, or to remedy the evils. The fact that these unhealthy conditions exist is proof that they have not been prevented. Year after year they have promised reforms before election, but have stood pat and defied all after being put into office. They have never kept faith with any but the capitalist, who put up the money to secure their election, and Mr. Harriman did not think the Administration kept faith with him.

RADICALS IN BOTH PARTIES

The foolish cry that the Negro cannot go into the Democratic Party because of its firebrands loses its weight when it is remembered that Mr. Vardaman has again and again denounced, vilified and abused a Republican President, sometimes in terms unfit for publication, but none of this has prevented our Republican President from appointing Democratic Judges, Cabinet Officers, Civil Service Commissioners, political referees and Democrats to every office within his gift.

If Democrats are good enough to be appointed by a Republican President, are they not good enough to be voted into office by Negroes?

I cannot see for the life of me why it is so highly commendable in the President to do everything that is in his power to win over Southern Democrats to the support of his policies, and, on the other hand, it is reprehensible and downright treachery on the part of Negroes to vote with the Democratic party in order to have that party change its policy and its attitude toward the Negro. It is the only party that can change the discriminatory legislation which has been enacted against us without a great political upheaval, amounting to almost a revolution.

Now comes forward the leader of the new Democratic Party and many of his supporters offering to help us if we will help them, and since the President of the United States is not afraid of Southern Democrats, surely we ought not to be afraid to reach out and take the hand that is extended to us.

Both the President and the Secretary of State had promised that the post of Minister to Hayti and the position of Recorder of Deeds in Washington would be given to a colored man, as had been the practice for many years. Upon the Pres-

INDEPENDENCE IN POLITICS 193

ident's refusal to make good his promise, I published the following open letter:

Honored Sir: In this open letter I desire to thank you most heartily for audiences granted and favors given me since your election as President of the United States; and, further, I thank the heads of the departments for appointments and promotions made in their several bureaus. There is a sentiment abroad that it is not the policy of the national Democratic Party to appoint and confirm Negroes to prominent offices. In the light of the following letter and the nominations of Mr. Patterson, Judge Terrell and Mr. Curtis, it is hard to believe that your excellency shares in this opposition.

Certainly the hostile Negro sentiment of some who occupy high places in the Democratic Party cannot be considered as expressing the attitude of the party toward us. If Democracy means anything at all it must mean the sharing in the government of every honest, intelligent taxpaying citizen, without regard to creed or color.

Surely this is eminently true at a time when every man of every race in our beloved country is expected to serve the colors in case of a crisis and is needed to insure "preparedness" for our national defence. It does appear to me that it should be the aim of the national government to inspire and intensify the warmest patriotism rather than discourage and repress the love and zeal of all citizens.

To be officially informed that Negroes cannot be confirmed in high federal positions, such as they have held under former administrations, no matter how worthy, is, to say the least, discouraging. We have waited long and patiently to know what our political status under the Democratic rule is to be in all parts of this country. In certain parts of the Southland a property qualification was demanded, and we met that, but to no avail;

then the educational test was required, and when our illiteracy was decreased 70 per cent. and when we had met the educational qualification, we were bidden to stand aside and wait a little longer, instead of being encouraged to register and vote.

In many places where we presented ourselves for enrollment we were ruthlessly turned down. It is well to understand that the Democratic Party cannot have the support of the Negro vote in the North, East and West while it denies the ballot to the members of our race in the South. For a national party to take such a position is unfair, unreasonable and untenable. As to the position of Recorder of Deeds, it has become a test case, and we are not now contending so much for the office as we are for the principle involved—namely, the right of Negroes to be nominated and confirmed in important offices.

We do hope, Mr. President, that you will not hesitate to make the nomination of a colored man to the office of the Recorder of Deeds or to one of equal importance where senatorial confirmation is required, for we desire to know whether it is to be the policy of the Democratic Party to accord to Negroes the same rights and recognition granted to other citizens of the nation, or, in other words, can the Democratic Party afford to ignore a half million voters on account of their color who are constantly increasing in numbers.

Most respectfully yours,
ALEXANDER WALTERS.

During the campaign of 1912, in response to an invitation to be present at a mass meeting at Carnegie Hall, under the auspices of the National Colored Democratic League, of which I was president, I received the following letter from Hon. Woodrow Wilson, then Democratic candidate for President:

INDEPENDENCE IN POLITICS

38 W. State St., Trenton, N. J.

My dear Bishop Walters:

It is a matter of genuine disappointment to me that I shall not be able to be present at the meeting on Saturday night, but inasmuch as I am cancelling every possible engagement, in view of the distressing assault upon Mr. Roosevelt, I do not feel that I can properly add others. I am fulfilling only those to which I have been bound for many weeks.

It would afford me pleasure to be present, because there are certain things I want to say. I hope that it seems superfluous to those who know me, but to those who do not know me perhaps it is not unnecessary for me to assure my colored fellow-citizens of my earnest wish to see justice done them in every matter, and not mere grudging justice, but justice executed with liberality and cordial good feeling. Every guarantee of our law, every principle of our Constitution, commands this, and our sympathies should also make it easy.

The colored people of the United States have made extraordinary progress towards self-support and usefulness, and ought to be encouraged in every possible and proper way. My sympathy with them is of long standing, and I want to assure them through you that should I become President of the United States they may count upon me for absolute fair dealing and for everything by which I could assist in advancing the interests of their race in the United States.

Very cordially yours,
WOODROW WILSON.

Personally, Mr. Wilson, since becoming President, has been very kind to me, as will be seen by further reference in this chapter. But so far as my race is concerned, I regret to say that he has failed to realize any of the expectations raised by his fair promises and sweet-sounding phrases about justice and equal opportunity uttered in pre-election days. His "New Freedom," it seems, has been all for the white man and little for the Negro. One can hardly reconcile his resentment of the manly presentation of the Negro's cause by Mr. Monroe Trotter, editor of the Boston *Guardian,* with the liberal sentiments toward the colored man quoted in the above letter.

Contrary to the precedent established by former Presidents of either party, Mr. Wilson has up to this writing never visited any colored school, church or gathering of colored people of any nature whatever. It has been the custom of the President of the United States to be present at the commencement exercises of Howard University and the Washington Colored Schools at some time during his administration; the administration of President Wilson, in spite of his assurance of sympathy with the race and the fact that they could "count upon him for everything by which he could assist in advancing the interests of the race," has been a notable exception to this pleasant custom.

Regarding the personal favors shown me by President Wilson, I may mention that in September, 1915, I was offered by him the post of Minister to Liberia, as is evidenced by the following letter:

Department of State,
Washington,
September 28, 1915.

Dear Bishop Walters:
The President is disposed to offer you appointment

as Minister to Liberia in succession to Dr. George W. Buckner, lately accredited to that post, and desires me to inquire whether this appointment would be agreeable to you. In doing so I would ask you to bear in mind, in connection with your reply, that the tenure of office of diplomatic offices is only during the pleasure of the President of the United States for the time being.

I shall be glad to receive a reply at your earliest convenience, and remain, my dear Bishop Walters,

Very faithfully yours,
(Signed) FRANK L. POLK,
Acting Secretary of State.

Bishop Alexander Walters,
208 West 134th Street,
New York City.

In my reply to this letter I stated that it was utterly impossible to accept this appointment, since I had decided not to give up my ministerial work for any outside position, no matter how great the honor or emolument. Again, I had recommended Counsellor James L. Curtis for the position, and I would consider it treachery on my part should I accept the position, were it possible for me to do so. I thanked the President for the honor and later Mr. Curtis was appointed to the post. And now that Mr. Wilson is re-elected to the Presidency, it is hoped that he will be able to make good to the colored people his pre-election promises made in the year 1912.

SPECIAL HONORS

1. February 16, 1915; appointed as member of Administrative Committee of the Federal Council

of the Churches of Christ in America. This Board represents thirty denominations and seventeen millions of church members in America.

2. June, 1916; election as honorary vice-president of the World Alliance for Promoting International Friendship through the Churches. The letter informing me of this honor read as follows: "I have the honor to inform you of your election as honorary vice-president of the American Council of World Alliance for Promoting International Friendship through the Churches."

3. February 12, 1916; election as Trustee of Howard University to fill vacancy caused by death of Dr. Booker T. Washington.

XVI

WORK IN THE UNITED SOCIETY OF CHRISTIAN ENDEAVOR

"'Go, then, and like the daybreak on the ocean
Whose roaring waves, tempestuous and grand,
Beneath that glory cease their wild commotion,
And turn to kiss with peace the wave-washed land.
Shine on the sea where human fates are drifting,
Till storm of tongue and social strife shall cease;
And in your light the Christ, with hand uplifted,
Shall walk the waves and say to tempests, 'Peace!'"
—REV. SHURTLEFF.

NO religious organization of the Nineteenth Century has progressed so rapidly as the Christian Endeavor Society, which was organized in Portland, Maine, Feb. 18, 1881. Starting with a few members, it has increased within twenty-five years to nearly 4,000,000; from one society in 1881 to over 77,766 societies in 1916. Indeed, its growth has been marvelous.

It was my good fortune in December, 1894, to be elected a trustee in this great organization (United Society of Christian Endeavorers), and from then until now (1916) I have been on the board. My association with Father Francis E. Clarke, the Founder; Mr. Willis Baer, first general secretary; Mr. William Shaw, Treasurer, and the other trustees have been to me both profitable and pleasant.

In 1895 the National Convention met in Boston, Mass. It was an immense gathering. I was told by the officers that there were 42,000 visitors who had come to the convention. Besides the great Mechanic Building, which held fifteen or seventeen thousand people, two large tents were erected for the accommodation of the people who desired to attend the services.

On Saturday morning, July 11, I spoke at Mechanics' Building, which was filled to its utmost capacity, over 15,000 being present.

The first address of the morning was made by Rev. C. H. Southgate, of Worcester, Mass. This address was followed by Hon. Elijah A. Morse, a very popular Congressman of Massachusetts. At the close of his address, Madam Selika sang, "Nearer, my God, to Thee." Then followed my first address before a National Convention of Christian Endeavorers. Subject, *"The Responsibility of the Afro-American in America."*

Mr. President, Ladies and Gentlemen:
There exists such a variety of colors among us that we have had considerable difficulty in selecting a suitable ethnological term which will take them all in. The terms "black" and "colored" have been found inadequate to exactly meet the case. There are other people in this country who are so deeply colored that they might with equal propriety be called "colored" Americans. Some who are forced into our ranks are so slightly colored that they can scarcely be distin-

WORK IN CHRISTIAN ENDEAVOR

guished from the pure white. The term "Negro" has been so perverted (some calling us "Ne-gar," others "Nigger," by way of derision) that it has become distasteful to us.

Some years ago Mr. T. Thomas Fortune, editor of the New York *Age,* the leading journal of the race, adopted the term Afro-American as a compromise term, which was at once accepted and is now in general use. The coinage is on the same principle as the term "Anglo-Saxon."

By the phrase "Afro-Americans" we mean Americans by way of Africa, or Americans whose ancestors came to this country from Africa nearly 300 years ago. The term is in no sense new; it was used by Rollins in describing the Afro-Assyrians. As a matter of fact it is the only proper term to use to rightly designate people of African and American parentage. Why should this whole race be designated by a term which defines color alone? Men and races are designated by the term which defines the country, the race to which they belong, and not by the color which distinguishes them from the rest of mankind. We are Afro-Americans—not colored Americans or Negro Americans.

The subject which I am to discuss is an important one, especially so in the face of the efforts to disfranchise the Afro-American in South Carolina, Virginia, Florida, Georgia, Alabama, Mississippi, Louisiana and other Southern States. The all-important question in the Southland is: "What is to be done with the Negro"?

There is a base element of untutored whites in this country that say, "Kill him out"! "Trump up false charges against him and lynch him without giving him an opportunity to prove his innocence, because he is becoming too strong numerically, intellectually and financially."

Others, a little better than the class mentioned above, say: "No, don't kill him; that will bring down upon us the opprobrium of all good people here and elsewhere; and again, the wrath of God will surely overtake us. But disfranchise him by legal enactments."

They have done this in Mississippi, where the law is that no one is allowed to vote except he can read the Constitution or understand it when read to him. The judges of election are the persons appointed to read the Constitution and to decide whether it is properly interpreted. Of course, that means the disfranchisement of the Afro-American, for no matter how correctly he may interpret it, it will be considered incorrect.

They are about to adopt a little different method from this in South Carolina. The declaration has been made that the whole race of that State shall be disfranchised by constitutional enactment; how this is to be accomplished remains to be seen. The present registration and election laws, which favor all the people, regardless of color, have been waived.

There are others whose consciences are too sensitive to approve of this plan, and they say: "Transport him to Africa." But after careful consideration of the ten million to be transported, the expense, etc., together with their unwillingness to be transported, they have come to the conclusion that this plan is impracticable; hence they are at sea as to what is best to be done; they would transport him if they could.

Thank God there is a class of right-thinking white people in the North and in the South who believe in fair play; believe in treating the Afro-American right, regardless of consequences, and leaving the result with God.

General Wade Hampton, of South Carolina, in a recent speech said:

"I have no fear of Negro domination, a cry used only to arouse race prejudices and to put the coming convention under control of the ring which now dominates our State. The Negroes have acted of late with rare moderation and liberality, and if we meet them in the same spirit they have shown they will aid in selecting good representatives for the convention. I for one am willing to trust them, and they ask only the rights guaranteed to them by the Constitution of the United States and that of our own State, and that ought to be allowed them."

I feel assured that every fair-minded person will agree with the ex-Senator.

The following appeared some time ago in the Richmond, Va., *Star:*

"A NEGRO STENOGRAPHER."

"In our last issue reference was made to the Negro stenographer employed by Messrs. Christian & Christian, attorneys-at-law, Chamber of Commerce Building, Richmond, Va. They may term themselves progressive by employing a Negro stenographer, but in a Southern community which is endeavoring to maintain the supremacy of the Anglo-Saxon race, especially when white stenographers of character and ability can be readily secured for a fair compensation, such action would be more properly termed 'retrogression.' This may do well enough north of Mason and Dixon's Line, but in this section it is a matter of importance to all that white labor be employed in preference to Negro labor in every position of this character. But the saddest of all is, that one member of this firm prides himself on his notoriety—on his standing as an ex-Confederate, and boasts of having shed his precious blood in defence of his country."

The firm replies as follows:

"The boy referred to was employed by us about five or six years ago in the capacity only of an office boy, for attending to our office, running errands, etc. He had previously attended our public schools and could read, write and spell very well. About two years ago, by his own application and diligence, practising on a typewriter which one of our firm had procured for his own use, he first learned typewriting and afterwards stenography, and has so far perfected himself in both that he has gradually become able, in addition to the duties for which he was originally employed and which he still faithfully performs, to do most of our stenographic and typewriting work. We have found him honest, faithful, efficient and respectful to us and to all with whom he comes in contact. We have of our own accord increased his wages as he has advanced in usefulness to us; and since he now suits us in all respects better than any one we know of, and as it would be an injustice to him to discharge him for no fault of his, we propose to continue to employ him as long as he suits us. If any one thinks less of us for pursuing this course we regret it, but their opinion of us about this will not affect our conduct in the slightest degree.

"Respectfully, etc.,
"CHRISTIAN & CHRISTIAN."

It is useless for any one to say after the expression of such sentiments that we have not true friends in the South as well as in the North.

Another proof that we have many friends in the South is the recognition which was given us in the Cotton States and International Exhibition, held at Atlanta, Ga., by the appointment of I. Garland Penn as Chief of the Afro-American Department, and the large amount appropriated for the establishment and maintenance of that department.

I am sorry to say, however, that the predominant sentiment in the South is against us in many respects. We are discriminated against on nearly all public carriers; no matter how intelligent, fair or well dressed an Afro-American may be, he is forced into what is known as the "Jim Crow Car," which is little better than a common smoking car. He is maligned and traduced upon the right and upon the left. No matter how hungry or weary he may be, no matter what his station in life is, he is not allowed to stop at a white hotel or eat at a white restaurant. In many instances our wives and daughters are insulted without redress at law.

On the 18th of June, 1895, an Afro-American girl in Alabama resented an attack made upon her by a white girl; the father of the white girl and some of his friends, hearing of it, went to the home of the Afro-American girl to whip her. Her father defended her by striking the white man with a hoe, whereupon the white man shot them both.

We all remember the diabolical killing of the five Afro-American men near Memphis, Tenn., and the shameful results of the trial. Does this show much progress in humane treatment on the part of the white masses in the South during the last thirty-five years?

We have been told that our color is the cause of the unfair treatment to which we are subjected. This is a mistake. A large part of the race is fair; they have only one-sixteenth part of Afro-American blood in their veins; their color is no protection to them against outrages. It is our previous condition of servitude. Because of this condition, caste prejudice exists. A great many people are disposed to treat us fairly, but are afraid of the opinion of others. This is cowardice, especially in Christians. They should endeavor to do right, no matter what the consequences may be.

In the East, West and North we are treated fairly well. We are given first-class railroad, hotel and restaurant accommodations; indeed, we are allowed first-class accommodation in most public places and on public carriers. We have the advantage of mixed schools. This I consider a fundamental advantage; the coeducation of the races is the most effectual method of eradicating race prejudice. Public sentiment in the North in our favor is far ahead of that in the South.

It is true in some instances we are shut out of the trades unions and kept off the public works, which is unjust, however; but this is more than overbalanced by the recognition of our manhood. In face of the above, what is the responsibility of the Afro-American?

I. UPON THE AFRO-AMERICAN RESTS THE RESPONSIBILITY OF PREPARING THE COMING GENERATION FOR WORTHY CITIZENSHIP

The indispensable qualification for worthy citizenship is intelligence. We are laboring diligently to educate the young men of the race, in order that they may be able to use the ballot intelligently. The perpetuity of our nation depends upon the intelligence of its voters. We are teaching our boys and girls to love our institutions, thus inspiring in them true patriotism.

No one doubts the loyalty of the Afro-American to the Stars and Stripes. He has been often weighed and never found wanting. The first blood which was shed in Boston in defence of American independence was that of an Afro-American—Crispus Attucks. Whenever the nation has called upon us to take up arms in its defence we have gladly responded to the call, from Bunker Hill to Appomattox. The Afro-American has mingled his blood with the blood of loyal citizens of the North and South on a hundred battlefields in defence of the Union. Notwithstanding the discriminations and outrages which have been perpetrated against him, he has never been known to take up arms against the nation which gave him birth and freedom. It is a part of the Afro-American's makeup to be loyal. Whoever heard of his combining to destroy property and annul law? If President McKinley in the next few days should be forced to call for troops to whip Spain, and I read the other day where the President and the Navy Department were considering the advisability of putting Negro soldiers in Cuba.

WORK IN CHRISTIAN ENDEAVOR 207

As an illustration of the loyalty of the Afro-American, I will relate a personal incident.

While abroad in 1889 I had the good fortune to be entertained in royal style by our European friends. One day, while sailing on the Rhine thinking about my entertainment, so different from that to which I had been accustomed in my own country, my attention was attracted to a beautiful castle. A few moments later a lady came to the window with something in her hand, when, lo, to my surprise she began to unfurl the Stars and Stripes. "Old Glory" never appeared to me so beautiful and grand as at that moment. I forgot all the discriminations and outrages to which I had been subjected in my own country; forgot all the magnificent entertainment of which I had been the recipient for four months; forgot my surroundings, and, waving my hat, I shouted at the top of my voice, "Hurrah for the Stars and Stripes"! In my heart I said: "America, with all her faults I love her still."

Ah, my friends, there was an outburst of genuine loyalty to the old flag.

II. UPON THE AFRO-AMERICAN RESTS THE RESPONSIBILITY OF SECURING HIS CIVIL AND POLITICAL RIGHTS

Our enfranchisement must be maintained. The doors of hotels, restaurants and other public places which are now closed against us must be opened. This can be achieved by intelligence, character, wealth and wise agitation.

1. Intelligence. No nation can be influential and great without intelligence. It has united continents, founded magnificent cities, invented machines, built railroads, tunneled mountains, bridged rivers. It teaches the minister how to properly interpret the Scriptures and win souls to Christ. It teaches the judge how to render a decision; the lawyer how to

plead a case; the physician how to cure a patient; the accountant how to keep his books; the farmer how to till the soil. The watchword of the hour is, *Educate! Educate! Educate!*

It is surprising what amounts we have given out of our meagre wages to establish educational institutions. We have contributed between four and five hundred thousand dollars annually within the last three or four years for educational purposes. We have 2,112,762 pupils in the common schools, colleges and other institutions of high grade throughout the country. We have 32,000 teachers and about the same number of intelligent preachers. Just think of these mighty hosts going forward and doing all in their power to prepare the coming generation for usefulness.

2. Character. The most important thing with us is character. Without this as a foundation, our superstructure will be almost useless. Our boys, and in some instances our girls, must be saved from the dram shops, the houses of ill fame, the gambling dens, pool-rooms and policy shops. The hope of the Afro-American race, as of all other races, lies in its character. Education and wealth are all right, and we must have them; but above every other qualification, if we would *command* as well as *demand* respect, we must possess character. This fact must be impressed upon the rising generation by parents, ministers and teachers. It will do more to solve the Afro-American problem than any other thing under heaven.

"To make our people strong in Christian character is to render them invincible in the battle of life."

Every race of this great commonwealth needs character, but the Afro-American, because of his unique position, needs it more than any other race. Upon us rests the responsibility of presenting to the world, as far as the Afro-American race is concerned, a virtuous and honest citizenship.

The work is a tremendous one when we remember

WORK IN CHRISTIAN ENDEAVOR 209

the ten million people with whom we have to do; still, we are not discouraged. With faith in God and faith in the possibility of the moral as well as the intellectual development of the race, we believe this work will be accomplished, stupendous as it is.

"We are anxious that every Afro-American in every part of this country should be made to feel, and as soon as possible, the transcendent importance of character."

We must change public sentiment along this line in our favor. I feel this to be our greatest responsibility.

3. "Wealth is a most important and powerful means of extending human influence in every direction. It is indeed a blessing to any people which will use it rightfully. It is not to be used for selfish ends, but for the accomplishment of noble purposes."

We are accumulating wealth rapidly. A little more frugality on the part of the race and a fair show in the business arena will afford us sufficient wealth to wield a mighty influence in this nation.

4. Wise Agitation. By wise agitation I mean an intelligent, reasonable, yet manly presentation of the discriminations and outrages to which we are subjected. We are not afraid to give credit to all who are friendly to our cause or who aid us in any way, shape or form, whether they be in the North or South. I would not have you think for a moment that we are unappreciative or ungrateful for past favors; neither would I have you think that we will be contented with less than our equal rights as guaranteed to us by the Constitution.

Agitation has been the watchword of oppressed people for the centuries; it is a cry which the oppressor has always endeavored to stifle. If we would have our wrongs righted we must speak out till right-minded people hear and come to our rescue.

Panoplied with character, intelligence and wealth, coupled with wise agitation, we will sweep the "Jim

Crow Car" out of existence, lynch law will be unheard of, and such a deed as burning a human being at the stake will be a thing of yore. Future generations will be unable to understand how such things could have ever occurred.

With character, intelligence and wealth we will not have to go out of our way to demand respect, for we will *command* it, especially if we exercise good judgment.

No one need fear Afro-American domination. Numbers and everything are against that idea. Again, the Afro-American does not desire to dominate; all he wants is fair play. The cry of domination, as General Wade Hampton has well said, is only raised to prejudice our cause.

SOCIAL EQUALITY

As to social equality, I agree with Bishop Haygood, who says:

"The social spheres arrange themselves to suit themselves, and no law promulgated by church or state will change the social affinities and natural selections of men. Men choose the circles for which they have affinity; seek the companionship they prefer and find the places suited to them. No human force or sagacity will change the social laws which bring men together or repel them."

I have great faith in the American conscience. It is on the side of liberty and fair play; all it needs is to be awakened. It is our duty to arouse it; this can be done by agitation. Once aroused it will sweep injustice into oblivion. Remember the results of the anti-slavery agitation. Over fifty years ago there was a class of people in the country who felt that slavery was wrong; and in my opinion the conscience of the American people is being rapidly quickened.

WORK IN CHRISTIAN ENDEAVOR 211

III. UPON THE AFRO-AMERICAN RESTS THE RESPONSIBILITY OF THE INDUSTRIAL TRAINING OF HIS RACE

One of the means to be used in order to become wealthy and influential is industry. It is not enough to be industrious, but to be skilfully so. The demand of the hour is for skilled labor, men and women prepared to execute their work in the most perfect manner. As a rule the Afro-American is shut out of the great manufactories and machine shops of our land; hence he is deprived of the practical experience which a person receives who has an opportunity to serve an apprenticeship under skilled workmen; and often when he has received such training he is denied an opportunity to exercise it.

This disadvantage was discovered some years ago and in order to remedy it we established industrial schools, where we might at least obtain theoretical training. We must have more such schools; more assistance from our white friends is needed in this direction than in any other. We ought to be allowed to enter all the industrial schools in the land, and where there are no such schools supported by the State they should be established at once.

Unskilled labor cannot compete with skilled labor, neither North nor South. In the past we have given certain positions by our white friends as the result of sympathy—not because we could perform the work as skilfully as others, but because of our poverty and oppression. The sentiment which actuated them to help us was a noble one; but that kind of sentiment is a thing of the past; now we are required to stand or fall according to our merits.

When anything is to be manufactured, machines constructed, houses and bridges built, clothing fashioned, or any kind of work performed, the most skilled workmen are required.

There are a great many employers who care but little

about the color of the workman; with them the question is: "Can he do the work?"

In some parts of the country there is a great deal of talk of whites preferring white labor and Afro-Americans preferring Afro-American labor, but I find in my experience that affairs are so mixed up in this country that that rule cannot be carried out to its fullest extent; if it was, we would often find ourselves in a pretty bad dilemma. Again, such a course of action is a racial sin and not in accord with the Golden Rule, which bids us to do unto others as we would have them do unto us.

IV. UPON THE AFRO-AMERICAN RESTS THE RESPONSIBILITY OF THE FURTHER ELEVATION OF HIS HOME

We can accomplish this by defending our homes at the cost of our lives, by honoring our women and protecting their virtue, and by giving them more liberal education and broader culture. Again, we can elevate our homes by strengthening and respecting the marriage bond.

Again, we are paying more attention to the training of our children, both in the cities and in the rural districts, than heretofore. We are teaching them to love the good, the beautiful and the true, and I am happy to inform you that we have made wonderful progress along this line. You would be surprised were you to enter some of our homes and mark the change from the cabin to the mansion, and you would be amazed at the culture and refinement displayed therein.

V. UPON THE AFRO-AMERICAN RESTS THE RESPONSIBILITY OF THE RELIGIOUS TRAINING OF HIS RACE

This will be consummated by well-trained, religious parents and teachers, and educated and pious ministers. Also by taking advantage of all the new organizations, such as the Christian Endeavor Society, Young Men's Christian Association, etc.

WORK IN CHRISTIAN ENDEAVOR

Our future happiness, usefulness and prosperity largely depend upon our loyalty to God and strict observance of religious duties. The stability of any people rests upon their adherence to religious principles. In Holy Writ we read: "Righteousness exalts a nation, but sin is a reproach to any people."

The Afro-American has always had the reputation of being religious, and this is no mean reputation. Some of our non-religious leaders deride us because of our religious proclivities; they claim if we had less religion it would be better for us. This is a grave mistake. No one can have too much piety. A person can have too much superstition, too much emotion, but not too much common-sense piety.

This address was well received. During its delivery I mentioned that I was a native of Kentucky and proud of that fact. Thereupon, the Kentucky delegation arose and tore down the flags which had been used to decorate their section and waved them vociferously, until the entire audience seemed to catch the enthusiasm, and united with them. It was an ovation of which any man might well feel proud. A few days afterwards I received the following letter from Father Clarke:

President's Office,
United Society of Christian Endeavor,
Tremont Temple,
Boston, Mass., July 24, 1895.

Bishop Alexander Walters, D.D.,
228 Duncan Street,
Jersey City, N. J.

Dear Friend:

I wish to thank you heartily for the genuine help you gave the Christian Endeavor cause at the recent convention, and especially for your excellent address.

I am sure it will help the Afro-Americans in all parts of the country. I believe that the far-reaching influence of these conventions will never be known in this world and all who helped to make the Boston convention memorable will receive the best blessing a generous heart can have—a knowledge of having helped others.

Faithfully yours,
FRANCIS CLARKE.

The convention of 1896 met at Washington, D. C. I was appointed to reply to one of the addresses of the delegates. While the convention was not as largely attended as the one in Boston, still, about 30,000 were present.

On the morning that I delivered the following address, a number of senators, federal judges and other representatives were present.

Mr. President, Ladies and Gentlemen:

I consider myself highly honored in being appointed to respond to the eloquent addresses of welcome to which we have listened. After the guarantee given to us at our last session by your honored President, Mr. W. H. H. Smith, that a feast of fat things would be spread for us in the Capitol City in 1896, we are not surprised at the royal welcome extended to us to-day.

He informed us that we were to meet in one of the most beautiful cities in the world. Said he: "There is more than 300 miles of well-paved, broad streets and broader avenues, shaded with 70,000 trees, thickly emeralded with more than 400 acres of public gardens, bordered with above 2000 acres of great parks, and filled with buildings, both public and private, illustrating every variety and combination of architecture and decoration." To all of which he invited us.

Besides this, he mentioned the great dome Capitol,

WORK IN CHRISTIAN ENDEAVOR 215

the National Museum, Navy Yard, Arsenal, Forts, Fish Commission Buildings, and other places of interest, and assured us that we would be welcome to them all. His statement aroused within us high anticipations; indeed, we came here expecting great things.

We are now ready to say, as did the Queen of Sheba to Solomon: "Behold, the half was not told us!"

I am here to represent the Afro-Americans of this great Commonwealth, and more especially the African Methodist Episcopal Zion Church, with its half million members; an organization which at its last General Conference, held at Mobile, Ala., in the month of May, endorsed by a unanimous vote the Christian Endeavor Society, and elected an organizer in the person of Rev. J. B. Colbert, D.D., of Washington, D. C., whose duty it is to see that a society is organized in every church throughout the Connection.

On behalf of the colored Endeavorers of the Nation, I thank you for your cordial welcome. In view of the recent discriminations at St. Louis by closing the doors against the colored delegates to the National Convention of the Republican Party, and the decision of the Supreme Court in upholding the Separate Coach Law of Louisiana, the welcome accorded to the colored Endeavorers and the appointment of a colored representative to respond at this time, is highly creditable to this grand organization; and it is gratifying to us to know that there is a great religious body which knows no man by his race or color, and whose cardinal principle is the Fatherhood of God and the Brotherhood of Man. If political sentiment was able to break down race prejudice and open the doors of hotels and restaurants in the city of St. Louis, what ought a great Christian body like the United Society of Christian Endeavor be able to do? I am glad that this Society is creating public sentiment in favor of the rights of humanity. Since it has God, numbers, wealth and influence on its side, it has nothing to fear.

If there is any class of citizens who are entitled to a cordial welcome to the Nation's Capital, it is the Afro-Americans, for they have suffered most at the hands of the lawmakers of the Nation.

It was within the walls of our great Capitol that the chains of slavery were tightened upon our wrists and ankles by legal enactments. It was here that compromises were made in order to extend slavery. It was in this city the Supreme Court rendered a decision that the Negro had no rights which a white man was bound to respect. It was here that laws were enacted to increase his ignorance and degradation, and to encourage in him immorality.

Yet when the old Flag, waving from the dome of the Capitol, was in peril, and when it appeared that the Nation would be rent in twain for ever, in that hour the Negro rose in his might, grasped his musket, rushed to the rescue of "Old Glory," and by his heroism and valor saved the fortunes of the day. Have we not merited a hearty welcome?

After much blood had been shed and treasure spent, it was from the Executive Mansion in this city that the immortal Lincoln issued his famous Proclamation liberating 4,000,000 human beings held as chattels.

After 240 years of hardships and unrequited toil I thank the Lord that it was under yonder dome we were enfranchised and given the rights of citizenship. Since that time we have made marvelous progress in religion, intelligence, morality and wealth. We have erected magnificent churches, founded splendid schools, and built handsome residences; accumulated nearly $300,-000,000 worth of property, have filled some of the most important positions in the gift of the Nation, and proved ourselves worthy citizens.

As a race we have heard your bugle call to spiritual arms, and hearing, have come to the rescue, as we did in 1862, from the rice swamps of South Carolina, the cotton fields of Mississippi, Louisiana and Alabama;

from the Everglades of Florida and from the tobacco plantations of Virginia; from the East, West, North and South we come as a reinforcement, to unite with you in order to achieve as great a victory as before, by rescuing our Sabbath from desecration, by saving our homes from the monster intemperance, our government from the clutches of boodlers, the ballot box from fraud and voters from intimidation.

On behalf of the Trustees of the United Society of Christian Endeavor I thank you for your royal welcome. We have gathered here from all quarters of the globe to do honor to the King of heaven, and by our songs, prayers and addresses inspire the citizens of Washington and the churches throughout the nation to higher aims and nobler endeavors. We come to aid in making Washington a better city and the officials therein, whether municipal or national, better rulers and legislators.

Our mighty host, with Christ as Chief Commander, the Cross our standard, and with our Faithful Father Clarke, loving and courageous Baer, earnest Shaw, Smith and others as Lieutenants, will march on to victory.

We have faith in the ultimate success of Christianity; faith in its power to cleanse the heart from sin and to save to the uttermost. We believe there is power in the cross of Jesus to overthrow all kinds of wickedness. Aye, more; we believe there is enough spiritual dynamite in heaven's magazine to blow the rum traffic from its entrenchments and to utterly destroy it.

Let the votaries of the Lord Jesus unite against the brothels and they will discover enough power on their side to close them up, and sufficient efficacy in the blood of Jesus to regenerate the most abject wretch who inhabits them.

We believe that Christianity has power to banish bribery and all manner of political corruption from our fair land. We will not cease to contend for reforms in municipal, state and national affairs until a reign of righteous government prevails.

We come with torches of Godly enthusiasm, hoping to shed additional spiritual light at the Nation's Capital. We hope while here by our inspired enthusiasm to fan the smouldering religious fires into a mighty flame. We have come to urge aggressive work along all religious and moral lines. We are here to speak out against religious intolerance. Our cry is: "Down with religious tyranny! Down with denominational bigotry! Up with United Christianity! Up with Universal Brotherhood!"

Christian Endeavor stands for the church, for the home and for the State. It stands for morality *versus* immorality; for honesty *versus* dishonesty; for sobriety *versus* sensuality; for all that is grand, noble and good in life and in death.

Our principle, "For Christ and the Church," was never more talismanic than now.

Again I thank you for your warm and cordial welcome.

XVII

ADDRESS AT ALEXANDRA PALACE, LONDON

SINCE 1895 I have been given a prominent place on the program of our National Convention. At the World's Christian Endeavor Convention held at Alexandra Palace, London, England, in 1890, I was appointed to deliver one of the principal addresses. Forty thousand people were present. The subject I chose was "The Minister's Responsibility and Care of the Young," and the address was as follows:

Mr. Chairman and Fellow Endeavorers:
 I consider myself highly honored and especially favored in being invited to deliver an address before this intelligent body of Christians. I am very sorry that we were delayed in getting here.
 We were first of all delayed in our journey by the Hoboken holocaust, in which over three hundred lives were lost and ten million dollars' worth of property destroyed by fire. In that catastrophe the *Scale,* on which we were to have sailed, three days after the fire occurred, was burned to the water's edge. This, as you have doubtless already heard, upset all the transpor-

tation plans of our managers, and forced them to make different arrangements.

After taking the good ship *Vancouver,* which sailed from Montreal, Canada, July 7, and should have arrived at Liverpool on the morning of the 16th, we lost twenty-four hours by a two days' fog. After all we are grateful to our Heavenly Father that we have at last arrived safe and sound. While on board, we held a daily service at 3 o'clock P.M., and I am sure with profit to all on board who attended the meetings. I was greatly benefited by the Christian fellowship of the believers who were on board. I am glad that none of our company of ministers was so unfortunate as a minister of whom I once heard.

He had crossed to this side some time ago, and a storm arose while he was at sea. The wind blew fiercely, the waves rose high and lashed themselves into fury. He became alarmed and asked the captain if there was not great danger of the loss of the ship. The captain said, "I think not; I have seen severer storms than this." He went to his stateroom, but soon after another wave swept the deck, the wind roared, the lightning flashed, and the ship seemed to stand on her end; the minister called on the captain again, and asked if they were not going down. "I hope not," said the captain, but to set the matter at rest for a while, and to keep the ministers from annoying him, he said, pointing to the trap door, "Do you hear those sailors cursing and gambling"? The minister answered "Yes." "Well," said he, "as long as they continue that you are safe, but when they cease to curse and gamble during the storm, the jig is up with you and all on board." The minister retired. About two o'clock in the morning, the storm grew fiercer, and the ship plunged and creaked as if she would break amidship. The minister could stand it no longer; he went to the hole, where they were cursing and gambling, put his ear down so he could hear distinctly, and mut-

ADDRESS AT ALEXANDRA PALACE 221

tered to himself, "Thank the Lord, they are at it still." Of course, none of our party would be guilty of such a breach of moral ethics—we had no storm.

Before I discuss my subject, allow me to give a few reasons why the colored people of America are in favor of the Christian Endeavor Society.

First.—Its system of religious training is peculiarly adapted to the religious development of our race.

The emancipation proclamation which was issued by our immortal statesman and President, Abraham Lincoln, January 1, 1863, unloosed the bonds of four million slaves. While we marched forth freemen, we at the same time marched out ignorant and poor. Ignorant because the light of intelligence had been denied us, and poor, because for two hundred and fifty years we had been robbed of our just dues. While we had many difficulties to face, we had three strong agencies on our side—God, influential white friends in this and our own country, and our own brawny arm. With this capital in hand we started out to make it in life. Since that time forty-five per cent of our ignorance has been removed by education. We have accumulated by our thrift and frugality over seven hundred million dollars in personal property and real estate. We have greatly improved our morals, and our mode of worship has been improved by the Christian Endeavor system of training.

The Christian Endeavor Society has enabled our young people who have been trained in the schools, and who are filled with new ideas to enter more largely into our religious worship, and thus improve our manner of conducting religious services. The half-singing manner of praying and preaching and the barbarous way of shouting are rapidly passing away under the touch of our Christian Endeavor hosts. All honor to Father Clarke, Brother Baer and other leaders of the Christian Endeavor movement.

Another reason why the colored people of America

are in favor of the Christian Endeavor movement is because it is Inter-Racial. While we have in our country some of the bravest and best white people in the world, we have a great many who are blinded by prejudice, and the colored people are the victims of most of these prejudices. We are disliked on account of our color and previous condition of servitude, for neither of which we are responsible. Color prejudice appears the more apparent when we consider that it is only displayed toward human beings. We never hear of color prejudice against a black dress, or hat, or coat; indeed, they are generally preferred. Black horses and dogs are considered beautiful animals, and are generally favorites, but when it comes to a black man, or woman, some of our folks will have none of it; but we are gradually being educated out of such foolishness.

As to our previous condition of servitude, we are not the only people who have been slaves. The ancestors of our Anglo-Saxon brethren were once slaves. The Hebrews were enslaved by the Egyptians for four hundred and thirty years. There are very few nations on the stage of action to-day who at some time in their history were not slaves. I am afraid that a great deal of the prejudice against us grows out of the belief that the Negro by nature is an inferior being. They seem to have forgotten the fact that the entire human family came from one stock, Adam and Eve being the ancestors of the whole race of mankind.

We read in the Scriptures that man called his wife's name "Eve," because she was the mother of all living. Again we read, "God hath made of one blood all nations of men to dwell on all the face of the earth." Therefore, in the language of our Endeavor motto, "We all are brethren."

To deny this fundamental truth is to renounce the Scriptures, for they are filled with the doctrine of the Fatherhood of God and the Brotherhood of Man. Since there can be no doubt as to our equality by nature

ADDRESS AT ALEXANDRA PALACE 223

with the other members of the human family, we should be accorded equally with them our God-given rights. The inculcation of this principle is what the Christian Endeavor Society is doing on our side of the water.

The United Society of Christian Endeavor knows no race or color. It can never draw the color line. If it did it would have to exclude not only the colored people of America, but also the dark peoples of India, Japan, China, Africa—indeed, the dark races throughout the Universe.

This cannot and will not be done. On our banner is emblazoned so that the world can read, God our father and man our brother. It shall remain there for ever and ever.

We have always had true friends among the white people of my native land. In the dark days of slavery our cause was championed by such able and courageous men as Abraham Lincoln, William Lloyd Garrison, Wendell Phillips, John Brown, Charles Sumner, Lovejoy, Henry Ward Beecher, and a host of others.

Since our emancipation God has raised us up many friends; indeed, their names are legion.

Foremost among them are Father Clarke and Mr. Baer. The white people, North and South, have contributed millions of money for our education. They have given our fairest and most talented sons and daughters to labor among us.

The government has honored us with some of its most lucrative positions. We are holding municipal positions of distinction and trust. We have made marvelous progress along all lines within thirty-five years; we have reduced the illiteracy among us forty-five per cent; we have written and published 1200 books.

We have accumulated school property to the value of $12,000,000. We own church property to the value of $37,000,000. We own 137,000 farms and homes valued at $725,000,000. We have personal property to the value of $165,000,000, and have raised over ten millions of dollars for our education. We have 30,000 teachers; students in higher institutions, 40,000; learning trades, 20,000; those pursuing classical courses, 15,000; scientific courses, 12,000; business courses, 1800. Total in school, 1,500,000. We have 156 Normal Schools, Colleges and Universities in the South. We have over 500 physicians, 300 lawyers and 400 newspapers.

We are very hopeful of our future in America. We believe ourselves to be in the dawn of the morning of our peace and prosperity; with God and some of the best white people in our country on our side we have but little to fear and much to hope for. It was by the aid of the God-fearing and liberty-loving white people that we are freed, emancipated from physical bondage, and it will be by their aid that we will be emancipated from our civil and political bondage.

After they had freed us they did not stop until we had been enfranchised, made full-fledged citizens in theory, and we believe they will stay by us until citizenship becomes an actual fact. The sentiment of fair play among the whites is on the increase. The Christian Endeavor Society is with us in our struggle for all the rights guaranteed to us by the Constitution. This accounts for my presence on the platform to-day.

We favor the Christian Endeavor Society because it stands for the deepening of the spiritual life. We live in an age of looseness of morals in church and state; an age in which men call license liberty; an age in which Bible truth is so distorted as to make men believe that they can commit all manner of sin with impunity so long as they believe in Christ; many believe to accept the righteousness of Christ is to have none of their own. They seem to have forgotten that the object of Christ's coming into the world was to save them from their sins. That the whole plan of salvation is the complete restoration of mankind to the image of God. Purity of life is one of the indispensable

ADDRESS AT ALEXANDRA PALACE 225

requisites for happiness and effectual service. It gives confidence and lends wings to faith and prayer. It was the theme of patriarchs, prophets, apostles and reformers. St. Paul urged it in all his Epistles.

We love the Christian Endeavor Society because it stands for Christian unity.

If there is one thing above another that has weakened the Christian Church in its work of soul saving and developing of character, it is the denominational strife which has been kept up for years in one form or another.

But, thank the Lord, it is rapidly disappearing before the flood tide of Christian unity, put in motion by the Christian Endeavor Society. I now come to the subject assigned to me by the committee:

"THE MINISTER'S RESPONSIBILITY AND CARE FOR THE YOUNG"

It is hardly necessary in this presence to stop to define the term "responsibility," but I will add in brief that Dr. Noah Webster says: "It is a state of accountability; it is being answerable, as for a trust or for an office, or debt. That for which any one is accountable or responsible." Grave, indeed, is ministerial responsibility. The minister is not only answerable to those who are committed to his charge, but he is alike answerable to the searcher of all hearts. I am here reminded of the impressive words of our ordination ceremony. Have always, therefore, printed in your remembrance how great a treasure is committed to your charge. For they have all been committed to your hands, who are the sheep of Christ, which he bought with His life, and for whom He shed His blood, and if it shall happen the same church or any member thereof do take hindrance or hurt by reason of your negligence, ye know the greatness of the fault, and also the horrible punishment that will ensue. Great, great is the responsibility of the ministry to the young.

Some of the essential qualifications on the part of the ministry for the training of the young.

I. The first essential element is love for the young. This means an earnest and longing desire to have them saved to serve.

We cannot make much headway in preparing strong men and women to do mighty work in the future if we do not love them intensely.

They must have our genuine sympathy and hearty co-operation, and to give this freely we must have a burning desire to save them.

We must have an experimental knowledge of the things which we are to teach. If we are to lead them to Christ, who is the world's ideal, to do it successfully we must have knowledge of Him; have a personal acquaintance. You must tell of His saving power, because you have realized its saving touch. He must be to you the fairest among ten thousand and the one altogether lovely. Your devotion must be so intense that you cannot help but speak of Him to others.

If you would warm the hearts of others, your own must be kindled into a spiritual flame by the baptism of the Holy Ghost. It is folly to talk of wakening others when you yourself are fast asleep. "The minister is to show to those under his care how Christ lived—to hold up His example in all trying circumstances in which He was placed, for He came to show by His life what the law required; and to show how men should live." And it is the office of the Christian ministry or a part of their work in preaching "Christ Jesus the Lord" to show how He lived, and to set forth His self-denial, His meekness, His purity, His blameless life, His spirit of prayer, His submission to divine will, His patience in suffering, His forgiveness of His enemies, His tenderness to the afflicted, the weak and the tempted, and the manner of His death. Were this all, it would be enough to employ the whole of a

ADDRESS AT ALEXANDRA PALACE

minister's life and to command the best talents of the world.

For He was the only perfectly pure model; and His example is to be followed by all His people, and His example is designed to exert a deep and wide influence on the world. Piety flourishes just in proportion as the pure example of Jesus Christ is kept before a people, and the world is made happier and better just as the example is kept constantly in view. To the gay and thoughtless, the ministers of the gospel are to show how serious and calm was the Redeemer to the worldly-minded; to show that He lived above the world; to the avaricious, how benevolent He was; to the vain and licentious, how pure He was; to the tempted, how He endured temptations; to the afflicted, how patient and resigned; to the dying, how He died; prayerful and pure He was; in order that they may be won to the same purity and be prepared to dwell with Him in His kingdom. We must realize the importance of the work which the young men and women of this age are expected to do.

Their work will be to carry forward the great reforms inaugurated by the fathers. To do this they must have well-developed, conscientious characters, strong to say "no" in the hour of temptation.

To train the young to do successful work we must study individual character; press the facts of experience, observation and revelation upon their consciences. Great care and pains will be required to do this work. As far as possible, we must deal with the individual, and this must be done in the home, in the public school, the lyceums, as well as the church of God.

Why should the Christian ministry give special attention to the young?

Because youth is the period when principles and habits are formed; it is the time to teach great principles of morality and piety if you want them inculcated. In youth the heart of the child is susceptible of lasting impressions for good or evil.

It is while the wax is soft and pliable that impressions must be made. Says Dr. Nott: "Youth is the most important because it is the first; and as such leaves its own impressions on all those other periods that follow in an endless series. Man enters on existence ignorant and impotent, but pliable and docile. The first impressions on his heart are the deepest and most abiding. Thus at the outset and during the inceptive process of moral agency a cast is given to his tone of feeling and his type of character. Secondary impressions of a similar nature only deepen the preceding, and carry forward the process of formation. Soon his taste receives a bias; soon his pleasures are selected, his companions chosen and his manner of life settled. Hence forward he advances, I do not say under an absolute necessity of being, but strongly predisposed to be for ever after what he hitherto has been. Habit renders pleasurable what the indulgence has made familiar.

The sentiments cherished, the maxims adopted, the modes of thinking practiced in youth, cleave to the man with tenacity of a second nature; and thus the web of life runs on uniform in its texture and woven of the same material to its close.

"Youth," says he, "is the period of fancy, of imagination, of passion, the period when the world appears most gaudy, and pleasure is most enticing.

Reason has not yet detected the sophistry of sin, nor experience revealed its bitterness. Even the worldly prudence which age imparts is not yet acquired; and all the avenues of the heart are left open and unguarded to the assaults of every invader. Now it is that health nerves the arm, ardour fires the bosom, and insatiable desires prompt to action. Now it is that a field of ideal glory presents itself, rich in objects of interest and replete with scenes of gratification; a field where every evil is disguised, every danger concealed, every enemy masked; where vision follows vision, and phantom succeeds phantom. Wealth, honor, pleasure, each big with promise, but faithless in performance, courts his attention and solicits his choice. Forms of beauty flit before the eye, songs of melody enchant his ear, streams of bliss invite his taste. Thus at the outset and during the inceptive process of moral agency a cast is given to his tone of feeling and of character."

If we sow in the hearts while the child is young the seed of obedience and temperance, we will more than likely reap harvest of sobriety; if you sow the seed of benevolence, you will have in the end broad and symmetrical men and women; if you inculcate the principle of truth, you may reasonably expect men of strict integrity and honesty. If you instil the principle of justice you can look with hope for righteousness; your fruit will be according to your sowing, and all admit that youth is the time to sow. It is the time to prepare the men of the future to do glorious service for God, home and country, or to be anarchists, socialists, and destructionists of all kinds.

If right principles are formed in youth, then happiness, peace and joy will ensue. On the other hand, if vicious principles are formed, then look out for trouble, misery or pain, woe, ruin, and external death.

This is why we should bestow so much pains on the training of the young. The wise king of Israel has said: "Train up a child in the way he should go, and when he is old he will not depart from it." And to the child he says: "Remember now thy Creator in the days of thy youth, while the evil days come not, and the years draw nigh, when thou shalt say, I have no pleasure in them." In youth the mind is a blank ready to be filled with noble or vicious principles. Go, my brothers, and help those committed to your charge to fill out the blank with right principles, teach them the lessons of love, truth, patience, temperance, mercy, justice, courage, and self-denial. See to it that they are cultivated assiduously and your reward is sure.

THE DUTIES AND RESPONSIBILITIES WHICH AWAIT THE YOUNG

Great reforms have been put in motion by the fathers which must be carried forward to a happy consummation by men and women who are being trained to-day. The children of to-day are the men and women of tomorrow.

The first thing to be fought is the Liquor Traffic. It is the duty of the young men and women upon whom so much care and labor have been bestowed and whose consciences are quickened to take up the temperance reform and fight the Liquor Traffic in all of its multitudinous forms, and especially since it is doing so much to destroy our homes, our governments and religious institutions. It is blighting our young manhood and womanhood. (A noted Colored Minister.)

Young men are called to fill the pulpits of those who have fought this nefarious business bravely for years, but who, on account of age, must come down from the wall. Their blunted swords have fallen from their palsied hands. O, young men, rise and take up the work where they left off. You are called to go into the school-room, both the Sunday School and the public school, where able champions who have fought nobly for years are about to lay aside their armour and you are to take it up and continue the struggle. Young men, you are called upon to take charge of the editorial chairs, where red-hot thunderbolts have been forged, and hurled against the rum traffic. Of you we expect more than of those who have gone before you. There is no agency more potent in creating sentiment against wrong and corruption than the press.

Young men, you are called to enter the halls of legislation, to occupy the seats of governors, mayors and

ADDRESS AT ALEXANDRA PALACE 231

counsellors; called to occupy the judicial bench, and to render strict justice, and to fight intemperance by legal enactments. You are called upon to take up the temperance cudgel and strike telling blows against intemperance. Young men and young women, strong in your manhood and womanhood, I bid you harken to the bugle call to duty; go fight this hydra-headed monster of wickedness in the homes, the churches, the social circle and places of business.

It is the duty of the young men and women who have received superior training to make war on bribery.

This seems to be an age of bribes. The eyes of governors, judges, legislators and municipal officers are closed by bribes to justice and right. They no longer see justice with the even balances in her hand standing before them.

Bribes have closed the ears of many in authority to the cry of the orphan and widow. It has sent the poor and oppressed laborer from courts where justice should have reigned, crushed and heartbroken. Heaven, your country and home cries loud to you to-day to arise in your might, and strike with a mailed hand bribery and corruption in high places.

It is the duty of the young men and women, especially those who have received special training, to fight to the death caste prejudice of all kinds.

You are called upon to lift up a standard against prejudice, wherever it exists, whether it be the class prejudice of India, which exists to the detriment of some of her noblest sons and daughters; or in Africa, on the part of the Boers, who took delight in humiliating the natives by forcing them from the sidewalks into the streets of their towns, and excluding them from their public places, or in old England, that is first among the nations of the world and whose history has been illustrious by noble deeds, in the frown of their nobility upon her less favored class, or whether it be in America, the land of the free and the home of the brave, where live some of the noblest and best of earth, in her oppression of the Negro and the Indian.

Her signs of prejudice are the separated coach laws, her separate schools, separate churches, and denial in some sections of the ballot to the black brother. Young men and women, you are called to help us fight this prejudice. It is the duty of young men and women, upon whom has been bestowed so much pains and labor, to keep inviolate our holy Sabbath. You have been strong to resist the onrushing tide of Sabbath desecration.

It is the duty of young men and women, especially those who have received superior training, to fight illegal and injurious trusts.

Combinations in business which have for their object the crushing and driving out of business all the small enterprises, the stifling of one's endeavor on the part of ambitious young men, who are forced to start in business life on small capital and whose aspirations to become strong and influential business men should not be crushed. Combinations which have for their object the fleecing of the poor, and as their end the driving out of business all but the capitalist, should be driven out of existence.

Lastly, young men, you are called upon to fight wrong and injustice of all kinds. You are called upon, like the illustrious knights of old, to consecrate yourselves to righting of wrongs. You are to strike in defence of those who are oppressed. Hear the Master say to-day, "To the work! To the work!"

XVIII

THE CHICAGO CHRISTIAN ENDEAVOR CONVENTION, 1915

> Then, speeding like full day through heaven's gate,
> Increased till all the earth was its domain.
> That figure was the grand prefiguration
> Of that new Era born of love and truth,
> Earth freed from night by dawn's emancipation,
> Emmanuel's morning in the hearts of youth.
> —REV. ERNEST WARBURTON SHURTLEFF.

THE Fifth World's Convention of Christian Endeavor met in 1915 in Chicago. The meetings were held in the Coliseum, and in welcoming the Chicago committee, Vice-President Grose said: "This Chicago Convention of 1915 will go down in Christian Endeavor history as one of the greatest, most significant and most successful of all the twenty-seven."

For twenty-seven years the presence of Father Clarke, the founder of the Christian Endeavor movement, had been the chief source of inspiration. Here for the first time he was absent. In the clutch of illness he tarried at Sagamore Beach while the delegates bemoaned the destiny which robbed them of his counsel and invaluable advice. His seat was empty, and to say that he was missed is but putting it mildly. Resolutions were passed and sent to the Christian Endeavor Sage, all of which breathed the spirit of reverence and devotion in which he was held. The following resolutions were passed and sent to him at Sagamore Beach:

> We, the delegates in attendance at the Twenty-seventh International and Fifth World's Convention of Christian Endeavor, representing over three millions of young people of the evangelical churches of the United States of America, in this opening session at Chicago, wish to assure you of our sincere sympathy with you in the discharge of the difficult duties incumbent upon you in these critical days as chief executive of the nation, and our earnest support in your measures in defence of neutral rights, international law and the higher law of humanity.
> We are grateful to God for your wise, temperate and firm leadership; for your ardent desire to preserve peace with all the world, so far as it can be done with due regard to those principles of righteousness which alone make nations worthy of preservation.
> Our prayer is that you may be divinely guided and sustained. May the consciousness of the people's approval and loyalty gird you with strength.

It was at this General Convention that the Christian Endeavor Society took high ground on the race question, condemning lynching, disfranchisement and discrimination of all kinds against the colored people, and pledging itself to do all in its power to bring the dawn of a new era of love and brotherhood between the races of mankind.

CHICAGO (1915) CONVENTION 235

The slogan, "A saloonless nation in 1920," was emphasized.

The following resolution was adopted:

PROHIBITION

We reaffirm our faith in the early triumph of national prohibition, and we again lift the slogan, "A saloonless nation by 1920." We rejoice in the coming together more and more of the temperance forces of all organizations for harmonious and united action against the common liquor foe.

We are grateful to Almighty God for the successful labors of the Flying Squadron of America, which in less than nine months penetrated every State of the Union, visiting every capital city and practically every other commercial and educational centre of the Union with the message of national prohibition. We are glad of the place occupied by Christian Endeavor in this campaign, both through the presence of a number of her leaders in the Squadron itself, and also by the vital co-operation everywhere of the young people themselves on the field.

We indorse the campaign now being promoted by the Anti-Saloon League, the Woman's Christian Temperance Union, and other kindred organizations, for the election to Congress of United States Senators and Representatives openly pledged to support national constitutional prohibition.

We commend the efforts now being made through representative leaders of all political parties to enlist at least five million voters of the United States who will declare the patriotic determination to support at the polls those parties and candidates outspokenly committed to State and national prohibition. No organization unwilling to assume a righteous attitude upon this paramount moral, religious, industrial and political issue has any claim on the support of good citizens.

But we do not confine our vision to this republic, nor do we limit our program to the North American continent. Assembled in a World's Convention and rejoicing in the anti-liquor triumphs of the Dominion of Canada and the United States, we here lift our hopes and our determinations beyond the boundaries of States and countries, and declare for "Universal Prohibition."

The following address was delivered by the writer:

CHRISTIANITY—THE SOLUTION OF RACE PREJUDICE

Dean Miller, of Harvard University, says, "The adjustment of the forward and backward races of mankind is without doubt the most urgent problem that presses upon the twentieth century for solution. The range of this problem is not limited to any country or continent or hemisphere, its area is as wide as the habitable globe." I quite agree with him that the work of the Christian Church of the twentieth century is the permanent establishment of the doctrine of the brotherhood of man. This is the meaning of all our labor agitation, the activities of Japan, China, India, Egypt, South Africa; indeed, all parts of Africa, and the struggle will not cease until the recognition of the brotherhood of man shall have become an accomplished fact.

THE UNITY OF THE HUMAN FAMILY

It is pretty generally admitted within and without scientific circles that "God hath made of one blood all nations of men for to dwell on all the face of the earth."

"There is not the slightest difference under the microscope between the blood of a Chinaman, Japanese, Negro or a white man. There is no such thing as blue blood, patrician blood and royal blood as distinguished from

CHICAGO (1915) CONVENTION 237

red—common or plebeian blood; we are all from the same stock, whether white, black, brown or copper colored."

Color is the result of climatic conditions and not the fiat at the beginning by Almighty God. Great as is the difference between the various races of man as to formation of skull, long or broad heads, size of their jaws, curly or straight hair, straight or projecting teeth, all have sprung from the one stock.

St. Paul's assertion that God hath made of one blood all the nations of men to dwell upon the face of the earth, holds good. With the same blood—and other things being equal—there should be equality of opportunity and equality of privileges and rights.

THE CAUSE OF RACE PREJUDICE

God in His infinite wisdom has seen fit in carrying forward the civilization of the world to select certain people to lead in the march of civilization, and misunderstanding their call and His purpose in selecting them for leadership, they became puffed up with pride and looked with contempt upon those who were not so well favored; hence, vanity is really the cause of race prejudice—inordinate pride is the root trouble. Says Kelly Miller:

"It has so happened that in the process of human development that the whiter races of mankind at present represent the forward and progressive sections of the human family, while the darker varieties are relatively backward and belated. That the relative concrete superiority of the European is due to the advantage of historical environment rather than to innate ethnic endowment, a careful study of the trend of social forces leaves little room to doubt of this fact. Temporary superiority of this or that breed of men is only a transient phase of human development. In the history of civilization the various races and nations rise and fall like the waves of the sea, each imparting an impulse to its successor which pushes the process further and further forward."

Civilization is not an original process with any race or nations known to history, but the torch is passed from age to age and gains in brilliancy as it goes. Those who for the time being stand at the apex of prestige and power are ever prone to indulge in such boasting as the Gentiles use, and claim everlasting superiority of the "lesser breed."

Nothing less can be expected of human vanity and pride. But history plays havoc with the vainglorious boasting of national and racial conceit. Where are the Babylonians, the Assyrians, and the Egyptians, who once lorded it over the face of the earth? In the historical recessional of the races, they are "one with Nineveh and Tyre." The lordly Greeks who ruled the world through the achievements of the mind, who gave the world Homer, and Socrates, and Phidias in the heydays of their glory, have so sunken in the scale of excellence that, to use the language of Macaulay, "their people have degenerated into timid slaves, and their language into a barbarous jargon." On the other hand, the barbarians who Aristotle tells us could not count beyond ten fingers in his day, subsequently produced Kant, Shakespeare, Newton and Bacon. The Arab and the Moor for a season led the van of the world's civilization.

"To condemn a people, whether that people be African, Japanese, Chinese or East Indian, to everlasting inferiority because of deficiency in historical distinction, shows the same faultiness of logic as the assumption that what never has been can never be. The application of this test a thousand years ago would have placed under the ban of reproach all of the vigorous and virile nations of modern times."

CHICAGO (1915) CONVENTION 239

THE UNREASONABLENESS OF RACE PREJUDICE

Since it has been shown that the race that is in the vanguard to-day is in the rear to-morrow, and how vain is its boasting, is it not time that the forward races of the present should take heed and profit by the lessons of the past?

To my way of thinking, Japan, with its keen intellect and aggressive spirit, is the rising nation, and who knows but China, with its ancient lore, may follow, then India and Africa, etc. It is God's way, and we should not despise the plan of the Almighty. I sometimes liken the plan of the ages—the plan to save the world—to a great army divided into battalions, and the army commanded by a wise general. This battalion and that is ordered to the conflict as their services are needed until the victory is won. This seems to me to have been done by the God of Armies. First, Shem was ordered into the conflict with the torch of Christianity aloft; and next came Japheth, and the conflict has raged the fiercer, and last will come in Ham with a mighty war-whoop, who will add the finishing touch to the redemption of the world.

We have something analogous to this in our late Civil War. White men brave and true entered the conflict; a mighty battalion from the East; another mighty battalion from the North; still another from the West; and another from the South. But the victory was not won; it hung in a balance; it seemed as if the Union forces would fail, when, lo, in the distance a black battalion was seen entering the field of battle, and adding their efforts to the white battalions already engaged; the victory was achieved; the Union was saved, and the slaves emancipated.

CHRISTIANITY THE SOLUTION OF RACE PREJUDICE

I admit that race prejudice is deep-seated, stubborn, and one of the hardest things to eradicate in all the world. The learning and culture of the Greeks and the Romans were unable to eradicate race prejudice. Even Christianity as practiced in the ages past has been unable to conquer it. But in order to know whether Christianity will in the future overcome and destroy race prejudice we must take a retrospective view and see what deep-rooted and gigantic evils Christianity has overcome and destroyed. Christianity met and struggled with the monster paganism—throttled it and strangled it to death. When the struggle began paganism had learning, court influence, wealth and prestige on its side, while Christianity had poverty, and was without learning or wealth, but it had the Christ-life—the divine life—divine love, an inherent force, on its side, and with these qualities it has conquered paganism.

CHRISTIANITY HAS SLAIN THE GOLIATH OF SLAVERY

When the struggle commenced slavery had the world in its firm grip; the masters of the time scorned the efforts of Christianity just as some learned men to-day in certain quarters sneer at Christianity. But on the side of Christ is time, truth and a vital force, and time, truth and this vital force are the conquering agencies in the world.

When the Pilgrim Fathers reached these shores and talked of overcoming the Indians, clearing the forest, building cities and making a new world, many said it was a dream that never could be realized. But it has been realized, and what a magnificent story the historian has to tell of the trials and achievements of American heroes in the development of our great country. When I study the history of the past it appears to me that Jehovah has throughout the ages carried forward His great work of reformation and civilization by the selection of one great truth at a time, and making it paramount until it found lodgment in the hearts of men.

CHICAGO (1915) CONVENTION 241

First.—It was the great truth of the Fatherhood of God that was put forward. Said Jehovah, "I am God, and beside me there is none else." "I am the Father of all living and have universal dominion." It required centuries to make the world accept this truth, but with the acceptance of this truth came the overthrow of ancient idolatry, and now the world believes in the Fatherhood of God and His universal dominion. But we must not forget the fact that it required centuries, mighty struggles, many heartaches before this truth triumphed.

Second.—The second great truth presented to the world was the Christ—the life and light of the world. He said of Himself, "I am the way, the truth, and the life." To Pilate's question, "What is truth"? Christ answered, "I am truth." Men said, we care nothing for your pretensions, and we will not have you reign over us. The struggle for the mastery then began at the beginning of the first century and has continued until now. It is admitted on all sides that Christ has conquered. The spirit of the Galilean is to-day the controlling influence in legislation. Christ is the inspirer of all the reform movements of the world of which we hear so much. In the midst of wars there are many plans being inaugurated for peace. The air is impregnated with them. Peace is the keynote of our speeches, the theme of our songs and the subject of our prayers, and who doubts that the great peace sentiment of the hour is inspired by the Prince of Peace. Christ is conquering in literature, and thus many of our masterpieces are about the Christ or in some way tinged with His doctrine. This is seen in the writings of Macaulay, Burke, Tillotson, Augustine, Luther, Shakespeare and Butler. Christ is recognized in poetry and song. Milton, Dante, Wesley, Tennyson, Longfellow and Whittier have written and sung in His honor.

The great painters have given Christ an exalted place. To convince you of this fact I need only to mention

Leonardo da Vinci's "The Last Supper," Raphael's Transfiguration," and Angelo's "Last Judgment," and in our own Tanners' "Resurrection." Christ is conquering in social and domestic affairs. Says Mendenhall, "It is true that in Christian lands there are institutions, monopolies, customs, partisanships which Christianity does not justify, and which it will overcome as its rightful influence is extended and obeyed."

Tyrannies, race discrimination, the burning of Negroes at the stake, oppression of women, ignorance, poverty and crime coexist with the Christian religion in different lands. Still, I am sure that the vital forces of which I have spoken, that mighty power which has uprooted gigantic evils, will overcome the above-mentioned evils. It is well to keep in mind that Christianity is represented by the vision of the river, and a man with a measuring line in his hand, seen by the Prophet Ezekiel. Said he, "Behold I saw waters issuing out from under the threshold of the house of God eastward, and when the man that had the line in his hand went forth eastward, he measured a thousand cubits, and he brought me through the water; the waters were to the ankles. Again he measured a thousand, and brought me through the waters; the waters were to the knees; again he measured a thousand, and brought me through; the waters were to the loins. Afterwards he measured a thousand and it was a river that I could not pass over, for the waters were risen, waters to swim in."

I understand the river to represent the progress to be made by the Christian religion, and the thousand cubits to mean a thousand years. If this is the proper interpretation, then it is well to note that the first thousand years of Christianity found the waters of progress only ankle deep, and that was about the extent of the influence of Christianity at the close of the first thousand years. In the second thousand years the waters reached the knees. This is the period in which we live, and it must be apparent to us all when we remember the evils which exist to-day that the waters or influence of Christianity were only about knee deep. In the two thousand years that are to follow, Christianity is to reach its highest development, and to conquer all evils. Christ our conqueror is riding on gloriously and has the ages before Him.

Third.—The third great truth is the recognition of the presence and work of the Holy Spirit in the world. He is counseling, guiding and controlling the affairs of men. We are just beginning to understand that the Holy Spirit is the executive of the Godhead; that He is the Eternal Spirit; the vital force in the world. We are getting our eyes open to see this great truth, and to see the need of the presence and power of the Holy Spirit.

Fourth.—The fourth great truth is Redemption. The sacrificial death of Christ to save the world—His atonement. At last the truth of redemption has found lodgment in the hearts of men, and a place in literature. Redemption is an established fact, and men are being saved through this great truth.

Fifth.—The fifth great truth is the brotherhood of men, and to establish this fact and make it workable is the work of the twentieth century. The brotherhood of man is the acme of the teachings of Christ. Like the other great truths that have triumphed, this truth will ultimately win. At present, the struggle is fierce in all parts of the world. Sometimes rights and privileges are denied certain members of the human family because of their color and previous conditions of servitude. With the dominant class in some sections, neither character, learning nor wealth count for anything. Being favored with leadership by Almighty God and because of such favors, they are filled with pride and will not recognize the equality of other ethnic types, no matter what their qualities of head and heart. But I am not discouraged. I remember it has ever been thus, but more; I remember that time, preparation and the leaven of the Gospel and an earnest struggle has brought about most happy results, and enabled the people that were once considered inferiors to take their places as equals.

HANDICAPS

With Oriental peoples their handicap is race rather than color; because they have not been favored with leadership and have not made the same progress that European people have made, they are considered inferior, and thus denied equality. With the native African it is color and race that are their handicaps, and being still further back than the Orientals in the race of life, it will require a longer time to achieve an equal place in the human family. It is Christianity and Christianity alone that is to level the barriers and give to these backward races their rightful places in the great Christian family.

AMERICA'S DUTY

America is the leader in present-day civilization. She leads in commerce, invention, education, religion, and social reform. She is given a wonderful opportunity to do service for God and humanity in taking the lead in solving the race problem on Christian principles. I am of the opinion that the purpose of God in allowing the black man to be brought to these shores and to become a part of this civilization was to prepare the white man, by contact, discipline, and education for world leadership in the spread of pure democracy and of the brotherhood of man. Equal treatment, fair treatment, just treatment of the darker races is the test of the white man's religion. When the white man can treat a Negro, Japanese, Chinaman, African, as a brother and accord him all the rights of a brother, that white man can pass—he is pure gold, and fit to lead

CHICAGO (1915) CONVENTION 245

any people and anywhere. We have all races here to be blended into one civilization with equal rights and privileges. The work is now in progress, and will be carried forward to a happy consummation. I am expecting a wonderful change to come over this American people, a change for the better, with all the discriminations, all hindrances and barriers against the Japanese, the Chinese, the Negroes, and Indians, etc., will be eliminated, thrown down, and all be considered brethren, dwelling together with the white man in unity and peace, and all the result of Christianity.

The Christian Church can hasten this great work. First, by being more aggressive in insisting upon the rights of men in the future than it has in the past. Heretofore the church has been more negative than positive, and this is why the work has gone on so slowly. Now, the call has come for a more aggressive struggle than heretofore. The pulpit should be called upon to contend for the rights of all men, regardless of race or color. The press should be more aggressive than heretofore. We only retard our work and delay our cause when we single out one backward race and make the fight for it. We should put them all together—Japanese, Chinese, Negroes, and Africans, and make a straight-out fight for the backward races, and it would not be long before we would see the results of our labor.

The first thing to do is to combine to stop all inimical legislation on the part of our government. This can be done by united effort on the part of the Christian Church. There are people that are so blinded by their prejudices that they are willing to have this country place a premium upon bastardy by not allowing a white man to father his child and protect the negro woman that he has betrayed. This matter has got to be dealt with in most fearless manner. As long as we wink at injustice and countenance immorality of any kind, there cannot be much real Christian progress made. The truth is, the times call for a vigorous opposition against all manner of sins. The Gospel is the remedy for all these ills. All we need to do is to apply it in the manner it should be.

We have seen the effects of Christianity in civilization and the industrial pursuits of men. We have observed its impregnation of literature and refining tendency in art; we have witnessed its initiation of reforms and its place in home life; but its chief excellence is in its effects on human character. Christianity must in the last analysis be judged by its ability to deliver men from sin and uproot existing evils—and this much needed work it is doing.

XIX

ECUMENICAL CONFERENCES

IT has been my privilege to be a member of three Ecumenical Conferences, namely, at Washington, D. C., 1891; London, 1891; Toronto, 1911. At the London Conference (held in Wesley's Chapel, City Road), I was assigned to respond, on behalf of the African Methodist Churches (Western Section), to the address of welcome. I did so as follows:

Mr. Chairman and Brethren:
To me has been assigned the pleasant task of responding on behalf of the African Methodist Churches of the Western Section to the most eloquent and thoughtful addresses of welcome to which we have listened. On behalf of twenty-seven bishops, a large number of presiding elders, 1,462,304 communicants, 1,821,468 Sunday school scholars and nearly 5,000.000 of adherents of African Methodism, I heartily thank you for your cordial welcome to old England, the cradle of Methodism, with her renowned institutions hoary with age; England, which has produced some of the greatest statesmen, orators, poets and preachers the world has ever known. We greatly appreciate the welcome to your churches, homes and hearts. It is eminently fitting that at the beginning of the Twentieth Century all branches of Methodism gather from all parts of the world in a

great reunion at the shrine of its founder, to confer together, and catch fresh inspiration for future service. It is only those who are devoid of sentiment and enthusiasm who do not believe in pilgrimages to famous shrines.

Who would not consider it an honor, as well as a privilege, to join the great procession which was begun centuries ago by the wise men of the East, to make a pilgrimage to Bethlehem's manger, there to present gifts of contrite hearts, sincere devotion and genuine love to the King of Kings and Lord of Lords, and there tarry until endued with fresh anointing from on high? What enthusiastic Protestant would not deem it an honor to visit Wittenburg, the birthplace of Protestantism? To stand upon the spot where Luther nailed to the church door his renowned thesis against indulgences, etc.? Or to visit Worms, where he met the famous Diet, and made his noble defence before Charles the Fifth and his legate of Rome, uttering truths which revolutionized the religious world? Americans patriots delight to visit Bunker Hill, to learn lessons of true patriotism by recalling the noble deeds of her heroes. There should be no objection to the enthusiastic Methodist family assembling at this mecca of Methodism to thank the Lord for John and Charles Wesley, and other founders of this movement, which has girdled the globe, and done more to ameliorate the condition of mankind than any other religious organization extant. It is perfectly natural, under the circumstances, for billows of gratitude to sweep again and again over hearts. For my part I am happy enough to indulge in an old-fashioned Methodist shout. We are here from all parts of the world to receive a re-baptism of the Holy Ghost, to be strengthened with power from on high, to stem the mighty current of sin which threatens to overwhelm us.

We have come to this mount of inspiration to tarry for a few days, and to look into the face of Him whose name is Love, until our love for sinners and desire to save them becomes a common passion. We have come to gather strength to contend against the rum traffic in all its multitudinous forms, corruption in high places, Sabbath desecration, and race and color prejudice. It is not my purpose to mar the harmony of this occasion, or embarrass any of the representatives from America, by injecting the color question. I have too much respect for my brethren to intentionally do such a thing. All honor to the Bishops of the Methodist Episcopal Church represented here—noble and fair-minded men they are. The grand old church which they represent has spent millions of dollars for the uplift of the Negroes, and given some of her noblest sons and daughters to prepare them for usefulness in life. Her sacrifices for our race have been many, for all of which we are grateful. As to the representatives of the Methodist Episcopal Church South, there is not a colored delegate in this Conference, or a Bishop or minister left behind, who has not the greatest regard for that peerless orator of Methodism, Bishop Galloway, to whom we listened with so much delight and profit this morning. We admire and delight to honor you, sir. The amiable and broad-minded Dr. Tigert has the confidence and love of us all. As much can be truthfully said of many other representatives of that Church.

We are thankful to the Methodist Episcopal Church South for what she has done and is now doing, financially and otherwise, for her daughter, the Colored Methodist Episcopal Church, a prosperous branch of our Methodism. Hence, what I am about to say cannot be construed as a reflection upon any church or representative here. But, since for some time systematic efforts have been made to destroy the good opinion which our English friends have of us, we would be untrue to ourselves if we did not, while on this side, take advantage of the opportunity presented to vindicate ourselves, as we may not come this way again soon. We have been represented as a race of rapists, and to my certain knowledge a few on this side of the water believe the report to be true. Our delegates while here, by word and act, are endeavoring to change that idea. We are not a race of rapists. We have criminals among us, as have other races, but I am glad to inform you that our preachers and teachers are doing all in their power to decrease our criminality. Of 191 persons lynched in America last year, only 19 were accused of assaulting white women, and only 11 of those 19 were proven guilty of the charge. The absurdity of accusing a whole race of being rapists when only 11 out of 9,000,000 people have been proven guilty of the crime within the space of twelve months. The English people have always been our friends, and we hope they will remain so. Even in the dark days of slavery, when our white brethren of America did not respect us as they do to-day, you furnished us a refuge from the cruel master and the fierceness of his bloodhounds. We can never forget your kindness. This is one of the reasons why we so greatly appreciate that welcome which you have extended to us. We trust you will not allow any slanderous report to destroy your confidence in us.

We plead for your continued friendship and encouragement. If a few mendicants of our race have deceived you, think not that they represent the best among us—they do not. Here are our representatives—men of honor, of probity, intelligence; men who possess the confidence of our brethren at home, and are worthy of it abroad. After an interval of twenty years we have returned to these shores to report the numerical, spiritual and moral progress of African Methodism; and here to report the intellectual, financial and industrial development of the race. To our trust were committed two talents; we are of the opinion that we have at least gained two talents more, and we expect to hear from you the "well done, good and faithful servant." We have brought with us Presidents and ex-Presidents of influential educational institutions in the persons of

Bishops Lee, Harris; Profs. Atkins, Kealing, Scarborough, Jackson and Gilbert. We also have with us authors in the persons of Bishops Tanner, Small, Gaines, Arnett and others. And orators such as Bishops Clinton, Derrick, Smith, Williams; Drs. Phillips, Mason, Blackwell, Caldwell, Johnson and others. We have one banker among us, Dr. Moreland. On a certain occasion the great Senator, John C. Calhoun, of South Carolina, said that he would never believe a black man was the equal of a white man until that black man could read Greek and Latin. We have in our delegation to-day not only Greek, Latin and Hebrew scholars, but a man who has written a Greek grammar that is the text-book in a number of our schools and colleges; I refer to Prof. W. S. Scarborough, of Wilberforce University, Ohio. We are here to report our financial progress, to tell you that we have emerged from poverty to competency.

Our real and personal property is valued at over $700,000,000. We have moved from the log cabins to spacious homes, some of them palatial. We have a number of bankers and merchants among us. The colored delegation of twenty years ago was not blessed with the presence of a banker as we are to-day. This is surely an evidence of progress. Notwithstanding the discouraging statements which have been made concerning our moral and religious progress, it is with pleasure I inform you that we are steadily improving in that respect. The countenances of these delegates speak louder than any words I can utter of the moral and religious development of the race. We have made remarkable progress in our manner of church worship. The excessively emotional worship which obtained in days of yore is being rapidly displaced by more intelligent and orderly services.

The statistics of African Methodism will be presented by Bishop Arnett. And now may the spirits of the great Wesleys, of Clarke, Coke, Benson,

Fletcher, Arthur, Asbury, Simpson, McTyeire, Pierce, Allen, Varick and Miles hover over and inspire us. Best of all, may the Spirit of Christ, who died for us, guide us in all of our deliberations, and bring us at last to the haven of eternal rest. Again, on behalf of African Methodism, I thank you for your most gracious welcome.

The address was well received and published in nearly all lands.

XX

THE PAN-AFRICAN CONFERENCE

IT was the fertile brain of Mr. H. Sylvester Williams, a young barrister of London, England, that conceived the idea of a convocation of Negro representatives from all parts of the world. He presented his plan by letter to a number of distinguished Negroes in different countries, and after a favorable reply from them, he issued the call in the early part of last year (1900) for the Pan-African Conference, which was held in London, July 23-25.

The objects of the meeting were: First, to bring into closer touch with each other the peoples of African descent throughout the world; second, to inaugurate plans to bring about a more friendly relation between the Caucasian and African races; third, to start a movement looking forward to the securing to all African races living in civilized countries their full rights and to promote their business interests.

The meetings were held in Westminster Town Hall, which is near the House of Parliament. There were present the following representatives: Rt. Rev. A. Walters, D.D., New Jersey; M. Benito Sylvain, Aide-de-Camp to Emperor Menelik,

Abyssinia; Hon. F. S. R. Johnson, ex-Attorney-General, Republic of Liberia; C. W. French, Esq., St. Kitts, B. W. I.; Prof. W. E. B. DuBois, Georgia; G. W. Dove, Esq., Councillor, Freetown, Sierra Leone, W. A.; A. F. Ribero, Esq., Barrister-at-Law, Gold Coast, W. A.; Dr. R. A. K. Savage, M.B., Ch.B., Delegate from Afro-West Indian Literary Society, Edinburgh, Scotland; Mr. S. Coleridge Taylor, A.R.C.M., London, Eng.; A. Pulcherie Pierre, Esq., Trinidad, B. W. I.; H. Sylvester Williams, Esq., Barrister-at-Law, London, Eng.; Chaplain B. W. Arnett, Illinois; John E. Quinlan, Esq., Land Surveyor, St. Lucia, B. W. I.; R. E. Phipps, Esq., Barrister-at-Law, Trinidad, B. W. I.; Mr. Meyer, Delegate Afro-West Indian Literary Society, Edinburgh, Scotland; Rev. Henry Smith, London, Eng.; Prof. J. L. Love, Washington, D. C.; G. L. Christian, Esq., Dominica, B. W. I.; J. Buckle, Esq., F.R.G.S., F.C.I.E., London, Eng.; Hon. Henry F. Downing, U. S. A., ex-Consul, Loando, W. A.; T. J. Calloway, Washington, D. C.; Rev. Henry B. Brown, Lower Canada; Dr. John Alcinder, M.B., L.R.C.P.; Counsellor Chas. P. Lee, New York; Mr. J. F. Loudin, Director Fisk Jubilee Singers, London, Eng.; A. R. Hamilton, Esq., Jamaica, B. W. I.; Rev. H. Mason Joseph, M.A., Antigua, B. W. I.; Miss Anna H. Jones, M.A., Missouri; Miss Barrier, Washington, D. C.; Mrs. J. F. Loudin, London, Eng.; Mrs. Annie J. Cooper, Washington, D. C.; Miss Ada Harris, Indiana.

The writer was chosen to preside at the meet-

THE OLD MILL AT BARDSTOWN

THE PAN-AFRICAN CONFERENCE 255

ings; Prof. J. L. Love, of Washington, D. C., was elected secretary, and Prof. W. E. B. DuBois, of Georgia, was made chairman of the committee on address to the nations of the world.

The address of welcome was delivered by the late Dr. Creighton, who was Lord Bishop of London at that time. He said he was glad to meet the delegates and to welcome them to the City of London. He assured them that they had the sympathy of the fair-minded throughout the realm. He expressed a hope that the conference would be a precursor of many similar ones. Continuing, he said he was quite confident the great problems with which they were concerned would not be settled in a hurry, but still the movement to be inaugurated that day for the first time in the history of the world, no matter in however humble a way, was sure to go on growing until it brought a mass of public opinion to bear upon the questions raised. These would be of the most vital description, dealing with the future of the world, of which he was not then inclined to speak. For the first time in human experience the entire world had been really discovered, and a sense of human brotherhood had become a very real thing, and, magnificent as were the ideals it created, practical difficulties had to be dealt with. The conference would materially assist towards the accomplishment of this object if the delegates would place on record their experience of the views and aims of the colonial races. England generally recognized the weighty responsibilities

Providence had placed upon her, and her statesmen were constantly considering how to most adequately discharge them, and any help that conference could give them would be most gladly welcomed.

Responses to the most cordial and eloquent address of the Bishop were made by Hon. F. S. R. Johnson, of Liberia, and the presiding officer. During the session excellent papers were read by M. Benito Sylvain, C. W. French, Miss Anna Jones, Mrs. Annie J. Cooper, Rev. H. Mason Joseph, Francis Ware, Esq.; Rev. Henry Smith and others. The papers and addresses elicited great praise from the London daily press.

A Memorial, setting forth the following acts of injustice directed against Her Majesty's subjects in South Africa and other parts of her dominions, was prepared and sent to Queen Victoria:

1. The degrading and illegal compound system of native labor in vogue in Kimberley and Rhodesia. 2. The so-called indenture, i.e., legalized bondage of native men and women and children to white colonists. 3. The system of compulsory labor on public works. 4. The "pass" or docket system used for people of color. 5. Local by-laws tending to segregate and degrade the natives, such as the curfew; the denial to the natives of the use of the footpaths; and the use of separate public conveyances. 6. Difficulties in acquiring real property. 7. Difficulties in obtaining the franchise.

The following is the reply received from Her Majesty by our secretary, Mr. H. Sylvester Williams:

THE PAN-AFRICAN CONFERENCE

16th January, 1901.

Sir: I am directed by Mr. Secretary Chamberlain to state that he has received the Queen's commands to inform you that the Memorial of the Pan-African Conference respecting the situation of the native races in South Africa has been laid before Her Majesty, and that she was graciously pleased to command him to return an answer to it on behalf of her Government.

2. Mr. Chamberlain accordingly desires to assure the members of the Pan-African Conference that, in settling the lines on which the administration of the conquered territories is to be conducted, Her Majesty's Government will not overlook the interests and welfare of the native races.

3. A copy of the Memorial has been communicated to the High Commissioner for South Africa.

I am, sir, your obedient servant,
H. BERTRAM COX.

H. S. Williams, Esq.

Prof. DuBois, chairman of the Committee on Address to the Nations of the World, submitted the following, which was adopted and sent to the sovereigns in whose realms are subjects of African descent:

TO THE NATIONS OF THE WORLD

In the metropolis of the modern world, in this the closing year of the Nineteenth Century, there has been assembled a Congress of men and women of African blood, to deliberate solemnly upon the present situation and outlook of the darker races of mankind. The problem of the Twentieth Century is the problem of the color line, the question as to how far differences of race, which show themselves chiefly in the color of the skin and the texture of the hair, are going to be made, hereafter, the basis of denying to over half the world the right of sharing to their utmost ability the opportunities and privileges of modern civilization.

To be sure, the darker races are to-day the least advanced in culture according to European standards. This has not, however, always been the case in the past, and certainly the world's history, both ancient and modern, has given many instances of no despicable ability and capacity among the blackest races of men.

In any case the modern world must needs remember that in this age, when the ends of the world are being brought so near together, the millions of black men in Africa, America and the islands of the sea, not to speak of the brown and yellow myriads elsewhere, are bound to have great influence upon the world in the future, by reason of sheer numbers and physical contact. If now the world of culture bends itself upwards giving Negroes and other dark men the largest and broadest opportunity for education and self-development, then this contact and influence is bound to have a beneficial effect upon the world and hasten human progress. But if, by reason of carelessness, prejudice, greed and injustice, the black world is to be exploited and ravished and degraded, the results must be deplorable, if not fatal, not simply to them but to the high ideals of justice, freedom, and culture which a thousand years of Christian civilization have held before Europe.

And now, therefore, to these ideals of civilization, to the broader humanity of the followers of the Prince of Peace, we, the men and women of Africa in World Congress assembled, do now solemnly appeal:

Let the world take no backward step in that slow but sure progress which has successively refused to let the spirit of class, of caste, of privilege, or of birth, debar from life, liberty, and the pursuit of happiness a striving human soul.

Let not mere color or race be a feature of distinction drawn between white and black men, regardless of worth or ability.

THE PAN-AFRICAN CONFERENCE 259

Let not the natives of Africa be sacrificed to the greed of gold, their liberties taken away, their family life debauched, their just aspirations repressed, and avenues of advancement and culture taken from them.

Let not the cloak of Christian Missionary enterprise be allowed in the future, as so often in the past, to hide the ruthless economic exploitation and political downfall of less developed nations, whose chief fault has been reliance on the plighted faith of the Christian Church.

Let the British Nation, the first modern champion of Negro freedom, hasten to crown the work of Wilberforce, and Clarkson, and Buxton, and Sharpe, Bishop Colenso, and Livingstone, and give, as soon as practicable, the rights of responsible government to the Black Colonies of Africa and the West Indies.

Let not the spirit of Garrison, Phillips, and Douglas wholly die out in America; may the conscience of a great Nation rise and rebuke all dishonesty and unrighteous oppression toward the American Negro, and grant to him the right of franchise, security of person and property, and generous recognition of the great work he has accomplished in a generation toward raising nine millions of human beings from slavery to manhood.

Let the German Empire and the French Republic, true to their great past, remember that the true worth of Colonies lies in their prosperity and progress, and that justice, impartial alike to black and white, is the first element of prosperity.

Let the Congo Free State become a great central Negro State of the world, and let its prosperity be counted not simply in cash and commerce, but in the happiness and true advancement of its black people.

Let the Nations of the World respect the integrity and independence of the free Negro States of Abyssinia, Liberia, Hayti, etc., and let the inhabitants of these States, the independent tribes of Africa, the Negroes of the West Indies and America, and the black subjects of all Nations take courage, strive ceaselessly, and fight bravely, that they may prove to the World their incontestable right to be counted among the great brotherhood of mankind.

Thus we appeal with boldness and confidence to the Great Powers of the civilized world, trusting in the wide spirit of humanity, and the deep sense of justice of our age, for a generous recognition of the righteousness of our cause.

I have received letters from several of the countries represented in the Pan-African Conference commending the address.

A permanent organization was formed and the following officers were elected to serve for two years: Bishop A. Walters, New Jersey, President; Rev. Henry B. Brown, London, Vice-President; Prof. W. E. B. DuBois, Georgia, Vice-President for America. (I have forgotten the names of the vice-presidents and secretaries of other countries.) Mr. H. Sylvester Williams, General Secretary; T. J. Calloway, Secretary for America; Dr. R. J. Colenzo, Treasurer. Executive Committee: S. Coleridge Taylor, John R. Archer, J. F. Loudin, Henry T. Downing, Mrs. J. Cobden Unwin, Miss Annie J. Cooper.

The constitution adopted was similar to that of the Afro-American Council.

The gathering proved advantageous to the colored American tourists who had gone abroad to visit England, the Paris Exposition and other places of interest on the continent, in that it brought them in social contact with a number of distinguished personages on the other side whom

THE PAN-AFRICAN CONFERENCE 261

they would not have met except through the medium of an international and inter-racial gathering.

On Monday, the 23d of July, the conference was invited to a five o'clock tea given by the Reform Cobden Club of London in honor of the delegates, at its headquarters in the St. Ermin Hotel, one of the most elegant in the city. Several members of Parliament and other notables were present. A splendid repast was served, and for two hours the delegates were delightfully entertained by the members and friends of the club.

At 5 o'clock on Tuesday a tea was given in our honor by the late Dr. Creighton, Lord Bishop of London, at his stately palace at Fulham, which has been occupied by the Bishops of London since the fifteenth century. On our arrival at the palace we found his Lordship and one or two other Bishops, with their wives and daughters, waiting to greet us. After a magnificent repast had been served we were conducted through the extensive grounds which surround the palace. Prof. DuBois, M. Benito Sylvain, Messrs. Downing and Calloway, Miss Jones and others moved about the palace and grounds with an ease and elegance that was surprising; one would have thought they were "to the manor born." We found the Lord Bishop not only a brilliant scholar and profound thinker, but an affable Christian gentleman. I am sure our visit to the palace will be long remembered by the delegates as one of the most pleasant in their history.

Through the kindness of Mr. Clark, a member of Parliament, we were invited to tea on Wednesday, at 5 o'clock, on the Terrace of Parliament. After the tea the male members of our party were admitted to the House of Commons, which is considered quite an honor; indeed, the visit to the House of Parliament and tea on the Terrace was the crowning honor of the series. Great credit is due our genial secretary, Mr. H. Sylvester Williams, for these social functions.

Miss Catherine Impey, of London, said she was glad to come in contact with the class of Negroes that composed the Pan-African Conference, and wished that the best and most cultured would visit England and meet her citizens of noble birth, that the adverse opinion which had been created against them in some quarters of late by their enemies might be changed.

I am glad that so many of our ministers, educators and other members of the professional classes are making annual visits to Europe. Such visits are helpful to our cause. The Pan-African Association and the Afro-American Council, if efficiently officered and wisely managed, can do much for the amelioration of the condition of persons of African descent throughout the world, provided that they are supported in their work by the better classes of our people. Without such co-operation they are sure to fail.

If political parties, capital and labor see the need of organization, surely, as a race, oppressed and moneyless, we ought to see the necessity

THE PAN-AFRICAN CONFERENCE 263

of a great National and International organization. It is the aim and hope of the Pan-African Association, which is neither circumscribed by religious, social or political tests as a condition to the membership therein, to incorporate in its membership the ablest and most aggressive representatives of African descent in all lands.

We are not unmindful of the fact that it will require considerable time and labor to accomplish our object, but we have resolved to do all in our power to bring about the desired results.

The numerous letters I have received from different parts of the world commending the work of the Pan-African Association and the National Afro-American Council, the many local organizations which are being formed in various countries for the betterment of persons of African descent, the host of newspaper and magazine articles published by colored men in defense of the race, and the encouragement that is being given to our educational and financial development, are all evidences of a great awakening on the part of the Negroes to their own interests, and an abundant proof that the time is ripe for the inauguration of a great international as well as national organization.

Since these organizations have for their objects the encouragement of a feeling of unity and of friendly intercourse among all persons of African descent, the securing to them their civil and political rights, and the fostering of business enterprises among us, their growth in order to be permanent must necessarily be slow. But since great bodies move slowly, we need not be discouraged. As a race we have learned to laugh at opposition and to bravely overcome difficulties. Let us not be deterred by them in the future, but march steadily forward to the goal.

XXI

METHODIST UNITY

ON February 17, 1916, I submitted the following suggested working plan for Methodist union in the Harris Hall, Western University, Chicago:

I hail with delight the opportunity to meet with this goodly company of Methodist Churchmen who have gathered here to write another chapter in favor of the Union of American Methodism—a religious organization which has done so much for the spiritual, intellectual and material development of our Nation.

Methodism, through her ability, energy and numerical strength has taken a foremost place among the mighty agencies which have been used of God to give this Nation first place among the Nations of earth in inventions, commerce, and the propagation of the ideals of human brotherhood.

It has furnished to the Nation Presidents, eminent Members of Congress, able jurists, conscientious and capable State officials. Many of the professors in the leading universities of the land have been recruited from the ranks of our Methodism.

And yet, as wonderful in achievements as has been our Methodism, she has not been able to avoid the rock of disunion; but, like the Roman, the Anglican, the Presbyterian and other large bodies, she has had her divisions.

I am not sure but that in some respects her divisions have strengthened Methodism; but I feel pretty sure that these divisions have served their mission and the time is at hand for a United Methodism.

The Methodist Episcopal Church experienced its first division in the year 1791, when Rev. William Hammitt led a dissatisfied faction out of the church at Charleston, S. C., which organized and became known as the Primitive Methodists.

Being actuated by vanity rather than any distinct principle, the movement failed.

In the year 1792, Rev. James O. Kelley led a split from the mother church; this division called itself the Republican Methodists.

At first it appeared that the movement would prove formidable and become a rival of its young mother, but disintegrating influences set in and it never attained a robust growth such as some of the other offshoots did.

In 1793 a colored faction, under the leadership of Richard Allen, at Philadelphia, Pa., withdrew, and in the year 1796 another colored faction at New York City, under the leadership of James Varick, separated from the mother church; the former organized as the A. M. E. Church and the latter as the A. M. E. Zion Church.

These two factions withdrew because, as they stated, the proscriptions existing in the church at that time were insupportable and unbearable and were hindrances to their fullest development.

These two organizations retaining the doctrine and polity of the mother church have grown to be mighty forces in spiritual and race uplift.

They have attained to a membership of 1,188,608, with 8552 ministers and 9180 churches, supporting a large number of high schools and colleges, with property values exceeding $15,000,000.

And it would seem that the withdrawal of these colored churches was Providential and that their works

METHODIST UNITY

stand as their justification in their withdrawal from the mother church.

About the same time of the withdrawal of the above-named churches another colored faction left the Methodist Episcopal Church, led by Peter Spencer, of Wilmington, Del. It organized under the name of the African Union Church and later adopted the name of Union American Methodist Episcopal Church.

The strained relations between America and England growing out of the War of 1812-14 was the cause of the withdrawal of the Canadian membership of the Methodist Episcopal Church in America. This membership organized as the Methodist Episcopal Church of Canada in the year 1828.

In 1830 a number of expelled ministers, laymen and other disaffected members of the Methodist Episcopal Church formed at Baltimore, Md., the Methodist Protestant Church.

Their chief contention was for lay representation and that local preachers should be members of the general conference. It is still a considerable body.

The iniquitous system of slavery, said by Mr. Wesley to be "the sum of all villanies," was at the bottom of the largest withdrawal that the Methodist Episcopal Church has ever sustained. This division occurred in 1844-45, when thirteen of the Southern Conferences of the Methodist Episcopal Church withdrew from that body and formed the Methodist Episcopal Church South, an organization which has increased until it has attained a membership of 2,073,035, with a ministerial roll of 7203 and 16,787 churches.

Notwithstanding all these divisions, the mother church, peerless in her achievements and phenomenal in her growth, standing out like an impregnable fortress for manhood rights, and all that is best and noblest in life, is the wonder of all the Ecclesiastical organizations in America.

Many have been the efforts to unite the divided members of the Methodist family; but with two or three exceptions, and these of the smaller bodies, all such attempts have proven abortive. None that ever withdrew from the Mother Church has ever returned.

When one remembers the money, time and energy which have been expended to effect a union of the separate branches of Methodism and the resultant failures, the question naturally arises, what are the insurmountable obstacles which have prevented the success of the plans for organic union?

The question is often asked by the Romanist, "Did not our Lord Jesus pray that His Church should be one"? meaning by this statement the Roman Church as the one referred to. We answer, yes, our Lord did pray "That they all may be one; as thou, Father, art in me and I in thee, that they may also be one in us."

"The union between the Father and the Son is not a visible manifestation but a spiritual inference"; hence the unity spoken of in the seventeenth chapter of John is not an organic unity of denominations, but it is a spiritual unity which the Apostle Paul had in mind when he exhorted the church at Ephesus, "To endeavor to keep the unity of the spirit in the bonds of peace." It is a unity of love and service for the Master. The command for such unity is absolute.

As to organic union of Protestantism and especially the organic union of the different branches of Methodism in America, the only way to know the mind of the Lord in the matter is to note His leadings. All the signs of the times indicate that such a union is desirable and that the Lord is leading in that direction and that the struggle will continue until this union is consummated.

What is needed to accomplish this much desired end is more genuine Christianity; more of the spirit of love; more self-surrender, and a greater ecclesiastical statesmanship than we have had heretofore.

Says Bishop Merrill: "All agree that if union comes

METHODIST UNITY

it must be reached upon a basis honorable to all, and as the result of an inward persuasion which is so nearly universal as to be positively domination. Everyone will concede that the movement, in order to be either desirable or successful, must be as nearly spontaneous as is possible; the outgoing of a conviction rooted in Christian sentiment and controlling the consciousness of duty. When such preparation comes, union will follow as naturally as ripened fruit drops to the earth."

Speaking on the same subject, Bishop Foster says: "Patience, not haste; candor, not harshness; simplicity of aim will lead us to the true goal."

We need not expect organic union of any of the branches of Methodism so long as such statements are heard at the adjournment of commissions on organic union as the following:

"We did not surrender a point." "We outwitted the other fellows." "We have not lost a word out of our title." "We swallowed them up." "We have retained our dignity." "Why, certainly, we did not vote for the union; it was not honorable to us." Meaning that they did not get the advantage in the deal.

In many of the efforts for organic union there has been a greater ambition to excel in ecclesiastical diplomacy than there has been to effect a permanent union of the parties concerned.

If organic union is desirable, and I think it is, then any sacrifice that does not surrender or compromise manhood rights and the great truths of the Bible ought to be made in the interest of such union.

I have been a member of all the commissions appointed by the A. M. E. Zion Church within the past twenty-five years to effect federation or organic union between the Methodist Episcopal, the A. M. E., the C. M. E. and the Union A. M. E. Churches, and in every instance when the question of federation or organic union has been submitted, I have voted in favor of them.

In the year 1892 a commission on organic union

was appointed by the A. M. E. and A. M. E. Zion general conferences which met in that year, the former meeting at Philadelphia and the latter at Pittsburgh, Pa.

The commissions met at Harrisburg, Pa., May 20, 1892, and agreed upon a plan of organic union between the two churches represented. The main points of difference were noted, such as the appointment of class leaders, band societies, election of general conference delegates, dollar money (at this time the general assessment of the A. M. E. Church was one dollar and that of the A. M. E. Zion Church was fifty cents), the mode of the election of trustees and their duties.

All these minor matters were referred to the first united general conference of the bodies represented, which has never met. The name agreed upon was The African-Zion Methodist Episcopal Church. This name enabled the Zion commissioners to loudly proclaim that they had not surrendered a thing. The name, however, was submitted by Bishop B. F. Lee of the A. M. E. Church and received twenty-two votes in its favor out of a vote of twenty-four which formed the commission.

On leaving the church the late Bishop H. M. Turner declared that the hyphen would mean nothing to colored people and that the united church would ever be called the African Zion Methodist Episcopal Church. Notwithstanding the objections interposed, the plan was submitted to the quarterly, annual and general conferences and passed by the required vote, yet when the commissions appointed by the general conferences to consummate the union met in Washington, 1897, the whole plan was defeated and the union deferred.

It is with sadness that I state that all attempts at organic union on the part of the colored bodies have failed, as have all attempts at organic union (which have been many) on the part of the M. E. Church and the M. E. Church South.

It seems that we are not to have any organic union

METHODIST UNITY 271

until we are willing to take into that union all branches of Methodism, white and black, large and small.

THE KIND OF UNION THAT SEEMS TO BE DESIRED IN SOME SECTIONS OF OUR COUNTRY

I understand that the plan of organic union agreed upon at the last session of the general conference of the Methodist Episcopal Church South and which is to be submitted to the general conferences of the other branches of Methodism, contemplates the union of the white branches, with the hope that the union of the colored branches of Methodism will ultimately follow.

Of course, it is understood that the union of the colored branches is to include the colored membership of the Methodist Episcopal Church, when said membership shall have been organized into a separate and independent body, with its own bishops, general officers, etc.; such a separation as the Methodist Episcopal Church South outlines would result in a complete divorcement between the white and colored churches.

To secure such a separation would probably enable the M. E. Church South to unite with the Methodist Episcopal Church; but, while it would bridge the chasm between these two bodies, it would widen the breach and close the doors for centuries, if not forever, to a United Methodism in America.

A FEARFUL SURRENDER

In 1844 it was physical slavery that demanded of the M. E. Church a surrender of a Christian principle which she refused to do. In this, the year of our Lord 1916, seventy-two years after the separation and fifty-two years after the emancipation of the slaves, it is political and social slavery that calls again upon the same church to sacrifice her black brother on the altar of race prejudice, and this in the face of the fact of a half century of freedom, training in the best schools of the land with a moral, spiritual, intellectual and material progress that has astonished the world.

It seems to me too late in the day of this advanced civilization to ask such a tremendous sacrifice of principle on the part of the Methodist Episcopal Church and her black brother.

I for one am willing to continue separate conferences as we have them to-day, quarterly and annual, but with a general conference legislating for the united Methodism, granting to all of its constituent bodies and members equal rights and privileges according to membership; thus continuing the bond of brotherly love, making organic union a reality and not a sham.

HINDRANCES TO BE REMOVED, AS I SEE IT, BEFORE WE CAN HAVE ORGANIC UNION

The hindrances that must be removed before we can have organic union are:

First.—A willingness to enter more heartily and sincerely in the plan of making the Federation already existing a workable affair, with frequent meetings. With a stricter observance of the enactments of the Federation. In a word, we are to do more courting; we are to draw closer together and get better acquainted with each other.

Second.—A willingness to have a united general conference which will legislate and have control of American Methodism, white and black.

Third.—A willingness to submit all doctrines, church polity, non-essentials, for settlement to the first united general conference, with a solemn pledge to be governed by its decisions.